Starting Out
My Story So Far

ALASTAIR
COOK

HODDER

First published in Great Britain in 2008 by Hodder & Stoughton
An Hachette UK company

First published in paperback in 2009

3

Copyright © Alastair Cook 2008

A CIP catalogue record for this title is available from the British Library

ISBN 978 1 444 70978 0

Typeset in Nexus Serif by Hewer Text UK Ltd, Edinburgh

Printed and bound by CPI Group (UK) Ltd, Croydon, CR0 4YY

Hodder & Stoughton policy is to use papers that are natural, renewable
and recyclable products and made from wood grown in sustainable forests.
The logging and manufacturing processes are expected to conform to the
environmental regulations of the country of origin.

Hodder & Stoughton Ltd
338 Euston Road
London NW1 3BH

www.hodder.co.uk

Starting Out
My Story So Far

000002018442

To Alice

CONTENTS

CONTENTS

ACKNOWLEDGEMENTS

First of all, I would like to thank my parents, Graham and Elizabeth, for all their love and support, and for being an extremely reliable taxi service when I was younger! Heartfelt thanks, too, go to my family and friends for always being there for me. You all know who you are.

To all my team-mates with England and Essex I want to say it's a privilege to play with you all; and deep appreciation goes to the coaches and management who have helped my career so much.

Thanks are also due to Mike Martin for his expert guidance; to Roddy Bloomfield, the Don Bradman of sports book publishing, and Sarah Hammond at Hodder for all their belief in this project and their professionalism in putting it together; and to Paul Newman of the *Daily Mail* for all his help – this is the start of a good player/press-man friendship!

Photographic Acknowledgements

The author and publisher would like to thank the following for permission to reproduce photographs:

Mark Baker/AP/PA Photos, Bedford School, Hamish Blair/Getty Images, Philip Brown, Gareth Copley/PA, Adam Davy/PA, Anthony Devlin/PA Photos, Matt Dunham /AP/PA Photos, Mike Egerton/EMPICS Sport/PA Photos, Nigel French/PA, EMPICS Sport, Kieran Galvin/Galvineyes Photo Agency, Getty Images/ John Gichigi/Getty Images, Rob Griffith/AP/PA Photos, Tom Hevezi/PA, Julian Herbert/Getty Images, ICC, Ian Kington/Getty Images, Adrian Murrell/Getty Images, Rebecca Naden/PA Photos, Max Nash/AP/PA Photos, Reuters/Philip Brown/Action Images, Ezra Shaw/ Getty Images, Tom Shaw/Getty Images, Clare Skinner/ MCC, Jon Super/AP/PA Photos, Chris Young/ PA Photos.

All other photos are from private collections.

WHERE IT ALL STARTED

Everything was a blur when I made my Test debut, as an unlikely replacement in England's Test team, in March 2006. I had made runs, 60 of them, in the first innings of that first Test of England's tour of India at Nagpur. England were expected to do nothing other than submit meekly to a convincing series defeat, but now we were in the second innings and the pressure was on to score quick runs. Our coach Duncan Fletcher and captain Andrew Flintoff wanted us to push for victory in a match that everybody, except us, expected us to lose.

Funnily enough, I never felt under pressure in my second innings as an England player. We had been given no chance whatsoever of winning the match. I had seen Andrew Strauss and Ian Bell depart, and then Kevin Pietersen came in to smash the ball everywhere and take all the pressure off this callow youth at the other end. KP made it far easier for me to carry out the instructions to get on with it, although for a while it may not have seemed that way. I was 33 not out at lunch and 47 not out at tea – amazing, really, that I had managed to score just 14 runs in the afternoon session. In fact, we had put on more than 90 because KP was playing one of his unbelievable innings. I was able to bat solidly and let him do the job, at least until he got out, and then I was partnering Paul Collingwood.

Colly had scored a hundred in the first innings and was batting fluently again. I've heard it said that I was getting a move on to try to get to my hundred on debut before the close of the day's play, but I can honestly say that was not the case. I was told to score at four an over if I could and that was what I was trying to do.

I kind of knew it was my day when Harbhajan Singh spilled a caught and bowled chance off me. It was the easiest chance in the world, and once I had got away with that I was able to free myself up, whereas it usually gets harder and harder as an innings progresses. It didn't feel as though I was being selfish or unselfish, I just had to get on with it without thinking about the enormity of the occasion or the consequences of success or failure.

I remember running down the wicket and hitting Virender Sehwag back over his head to get from 87 to 91 and anyone who has watched my game knows that I do not usually run down the wicket to hit a bowler back over his head! I knocked the ball around in singles during the nineties because the field was well set and I found myself on 99 before I realized it.

The England team, unbeknown to me, had a sweep on for how many balls I would be stuck on 99 but I am not sure anyone actually won because I reached three figures off the first ball I received on that pressurized figure. It was a short and wide delivery from Harbhajan and I knew as soon as he let go of the ball that I was going to hit it. I didn't know if it would go for one or more but it was a classic hittable ball for a left-hander and I knew I would be able to push it for at least one. As it turned out I struck it for four and the feeling that followed will never be surpassed.

It was the best feeling I have ever experienced – a century on debut, as a replacement, as a twenty-one-year-old. I couldn't help thinking that I had proved I belonged and was worthy of playing with all these great England players, these Ashes winners, so soon after they had scaled the highest peak in the game.

It is very hard to earn respect at the top level and to show that you are not just another aspirant who will inevitably fall short of those exacting standards. I was not only an England player but I was a batsman who had scored a Test century, and on debut, too. It doesn't get any better than that. But it was only the start of a journey that has taken me from that unbelievable beginning through an equally unbelievable first two and a half years as an England player. This is the story of the journey so far.

1

HITTING THE RIGHT NOTES

I seemed to be in a bit of a rush to get going when I made my first appearance, on Christmas Day 1984. Mum and Dad were planning to spend the festive period with both sets of parents, first in Gloucester and then in Glamorgan. However, I arrived two months early to join my elder brother, Adrian, in the Cook family. So my status as a native of Gloucestershire was a bit of an accident. After that Christmas Day drama, I spent the first few weeks of my life in an incubator before I was strong enough to come home. Perhaps that was why I was small as a child, and it may even have played a part in my batting style because I did not have a great deal of upper body strength until I was pretty much grown up.

Home was the Essex village of Wickham Bishops, a very small and pleasant place to grow up. Later my younger brother, Laurence, arrived to complete our family. Mum's family are from Wales, where her dad was a steelworker in the Swansea area and Dad's family came from North Devon but moved to Gloucester, hence my place of birth. My parents met at university and settled in Essex, near the town of Maldon, when Dad began working in London.

We had a comfortable life but I wouldn't call it particularly affluent or middle class. I think when Mum was young, money was a bit scarce so she always had a good understanding of its value. She never liked to see it wasted, and still doesn't. If she sent us to a shop with 50p to buy milk and it cost 43p, she would expect to be given back the change. We never wanted for anything, and even went on skiing holidays, but I couldn't have gone to Bedford School, which I did from age 13, without a scholarship. I don't think the family finances could have stretched to paying for us all to be educated.

As you can imagine, with a family of three boys, without too many years between them, something was always going on in our house. We were all very sporty, as were our parents. Mum would try to send us to the field over the road to play cricket but, for some reason, we always preferred to play in our back garden, probably because the ball didn't go as far and we didn't have to keep fetching it. The boundary was the fence on one side and the flowers on the other while the greenhouse was at extra cover. During the summer, a cricket net appeared in the back garden, positioned to try to save the flowers, but it didn't always work.

Mum loves gardening but we used to cut the grass to shreds and there were bare patches on her beloved lawn where we would run through when we were bowling. Our pitch was 11 yards long – from the patio to the bottom of the garden – and Adrian would bowl at me with one of those balls that are softer than a cricket ball but have a seam on them, and I would need to be fully padded up otherwise it might have caused an injury. Maybe that's why I play short bowling quite well now. I used to have to face my older brother's bowling from 11 yards on a dodgy pitch – once we

2

bought a roller to try to flatten out our very own little Lord's, but it didn't really work.

Our games would go on all day during the summer holidays when we were very young. I would bat first followed by Adrian. Laurence had to do most of the fielding and would often get bored and go in before he had a chance to bat. Sometimes, if we were feeling generous, he would get a bat at the end of the day. We'd play for hours and hours.

Our village had a good sense of community and there was always something going on after school. The local tennis and badminton clubs welcomed youngsters and I can remember going there, as well as playing cricket, while football and rugby were also regularly attempted in the Cook household. It was a good, healthy, happy childhood revolving around physical activity. No Playstations or Game Boys for us in those days – we'd rather be doing the real thing.

I've heard the expression 'middle child syndrome' but I can't say I ever suffered from it. I quite enjoyed being the middle child. I was always very competitive, perhaps because my premature start to life forced me to battle a bit, and I would join forces with my older brother to gang up on my younger brother, or the other way round. I can't ever remember the pair of them joining forces to gang up on me, so maybe my personality was stronger than my body at that formative stage of my life. If anything, Laurence had it the toughest because I was always trying to compete with Adrian and perhaps he got left out a little bit. There was also a lot of fighting, again as you might expect with three boys, and I can remember us all having some good scraps.

It took a long while before we could compete with my parents at sport. They were very good at tennis and golf and would play to win. We used to throw a tennis ball around the house for fun. Mum would throw it at me, even while she was cooking in the kitchen, and I got a point if I caught it or lost one if I dropped it. There was always an element of competition, which was good for me.

My personality now is pretty different from my brothers'. Laurence is studying chemical engineering at university. He's highly intelligent and quite an original thinker, which could take him a long way.

Both he and Adrian are good sportsmen but I think I was born with better hand-eye co-ordination. We would all take part in local tennis competitions – sometimes it would just be us and a couple of other kids – and I hope I won more than I lost. Adrian is a more natural sportsman than Laurence, but Laurence keeps wicket for the Maldon club now, and loves cycling and squash. Adrian is more practical and he was the one I would turn to for any sort of mechanical help. I barely knew how to turn on a computer until I was 21. I've just never been one for gadgets.

Mum, who is a teacher when she hasn't been bringing up three boys, and Dad, a BT engineer, were fantastically encouraging and wanted us to play every sport available to us. They both love cricket. Dad played for Great Totham, the next village along from us, for years while Mum used to do the scoring. I gather Dad was a very good club batsman but he would never boast about how good he was. He is far too unassuming for that. Like me, Dad is right-handed but bats left-handed. An old family video shows Granddad trying to get me to swing a golf club right-handed, but I just walked around and hit it left-handed. I think I had seen my dad do that and wanted to do it the same way as he did.

But there was a catch to all this encouragement. If we were to pursue our love of sport, we had to go singing with them. My parents have always been musical and Mum belonged to a local church choir. Just as they wanted us to play sport, they also wanted us to sing and learn musical instruments. As often as I had a cricket bat or a tennis racquet in my hands, I also had a recorder. Choir practice was on Friday evenings with singing on Sundays.

My parents are not particularly religious people. It was the music they loved. If you go to their house now, they would have classical music playing. And it was music that led to the first major event in my life, something that led to me leaving my wonderful home environment at the very early age of eight.

I can clearly remember the choirmaster at our local Wickham Bishops choir coming up to my parents one night after practice and saying, 'He's got a good voice. Have you considered a choir school for Alastair?' That exchange meant very little to me at the time but it was one that was going to shape my early life.

My parents felt they must consider the idea and soon afterwards my dad said to me, 'Do you want to have a day off school? Let's go and visit St Paul's.' Well, I had never been to London before so it sounded good to me and before I knew it I was singing a song in front of the choirmaster at St Paul's Cathedral. And on the strength of that one song I was offered a place at the St Paul's Cathedral Choir School.

Now this was a seriously big deal. Not only would it mean leaving my little local school in Essex, but I would have to live at the choir school, which is right next to St Paul's Cathedral in London, and be away from my close-knit family.

You can imagine what a huge decision this was for my parents and they wanted my involvement. I had to decide whether I wanted to live away from home. My parents wanted me to have the final word, even at such a young age, because they did not want to force me into anything I didn't feel comfortable in doing.

I think their instinct was to take me straight back home but I was adamant that I wanted to go. I wanted to take this exciting chance and all that it would entail. Looking back now, I cannot possibly articulate why I made that decision but I knew it was what I wanted to do, and I knew that I would have the total support of my parents, who loved music even more than they loved sport.

As if going to boarding school was not daunting enough, the fact that I was going to a choir school meant that it would be very difficult to get home at weekends. That was the business end of the week if you were a member of a choir, when you would be required to take part in services. So the only real way to see your family was for them to come to London at weekends to see you, in between services. Even then, you could never go very far because you would be required to sing several times during the course of the weekend.

I don't want it to sound in any way an unpleasant experience. It was an extraordinary experience. And the fact that I was offered a place on the back of one trial must have meant that I was pretty good because the standard was unbelievable.

So off to London I went. I can remember my first day at St Paul's as if it were yesterday. First came the excitement of starting at a new school and travelling down to London, but then came the moment when my parents had to leave me there. I can see them walking away now. It was a difficult moment but it must have been much harder for them, even though they knew what an opportunity this was and how lucky I was to be chosen. For me, it was more of an adventure.

The thing that really struck me that first night in London was the traffic. All I could hear were cars driving by outside. At Wickham Bishops you never heard a single car going past the houses at night. During those first few nights in this strange new environment, there were certainly some tears. I would wake up and find myself in a bunk bed in a dormitory of 18 people and think, 'Where am I?'

And so began my new life. As part of the St Paul's Cathedral choir I would get up at 7 a.m., have breakfast and be at practice by 7.45. We would sing for an hour before a full day at school and then have another hour's practice from 4 p.m. to 5 p.m. Then we would have a service from 5 p.m. to 6 p.m., homework from 6.30 to 8 and bed at 9 p.m. We sang a lot on Saturdays and Sundays. Firstly, we had an hour and a half's rehearsal on a Saturday morning, then our parents would arrive to take us to lunch, and we'd have a service on Saturday evening. Sundays consisted of three services before our parents were allowed to take us to dinner. So we saw our parents just twice a week and never in our home environment. It was a demanding routine, one that stretched to around 25 hours of singing a week on top of the normal school week.

That first year at St Paul's, though, I was on probation. The regime wasn't quite so stringent for the eight-year-olds. In our year, we were just feeling our way. We had to go to all the choir practices but we didn't sing in all the services. We followed the music and learnt the ropes while the 13-year-olds, the ones who had been through the whole cycle, kind of dragged us along. We also had a few weekends off.

The longer I was at St Paul's, the more amazing it became. I went to Brazil to sing, and to Holland, and we sang in huge television services. I was a treble, just a foot soldier, really. The standard was unreal and I never stood out. I was a 'Steady Eddie' – reliable. I never missed any services or anything like that, and I got to sing with some of the best in the world, including Dame Kiri Te Kanawa, and with all the major orchestras. You couldn't get to a higher level in music.

The thing was, you were never allowed to make a mistake. The highest standards were expected as a matter of course, which meant that concentration was immense. Even at the smallest service on a Monday in front of 30 people, the choirmaster, John Scott, would settle for nothing less than the best. That instilled a lot of discipline in me. He always got the best out of us. If anyone made a mistake, it would ruin the whole service for the choirmaster, so he would never tolerate it if you were out of tune or hit a wrong note. He would only ever remember the bad things, nothing of the good that formed the bulk of the service. I can remember messing up just one piece, but I messed it up terribly. We never sang it again after that. It was as though one mistake was enough to render the whole thing worthless.

We would sing for all sorts of people. Music experts would travel from all over the place to come to hear us sing, and there were a lot of tourists, of course, not to mention those who came for the whole religious experience, not just the music. Sometimes we would sing to a few hundred people but often the cathedral was packed with more than 2,000 – early experience of playing to a big, demanding audience.

The cathedral itself is an extraordinary place. It has something like an eight or nine-second echo, which actually affects the way you sing. We had to sing a bit slower because of it. As a child, being there every day made me immune to the cathedral's attractions, but I went back about a year ago and it was awesome. I found it hard to comprehend that I had actually sung there, day in and day out. I suppose, when you're young, you tend to take things in your stride, and I didn't appreciate what a special place it is. It was certainly special for my parents, that's for sure.

Once I had been there for a while it became a bit repetitious, a music cycle. The same services came around about twice a year, so by the time of my third and fourth years I had seen it all before. At that stage, you were expected to be able to sing in a particular service without having to practise. All the real effort went into the major services and concerts, which came along every two weeks or so.

There were just eight boys in my year, but if you replicated that from the eight-year-olds to the 13-year-olds, you ended up with quite a big choir. For most of the time, 12 or 13 lead singers carried the load and took everyone else along with them. I was never one of the star soloists but I did sing a solo once on a St Paul's choir CD. In all, I must have sung on about 15 recordings, and there is one out there somewhere with me as a soloist, but I wouldn't pretend that you can pick me out!

At times it was hard. Generally, life was fine while I was at school and so busy, but when I got home, during the school holidays, I would find it tough to think about going back again, but I have no regrets. I think my five years at St Paul's played a huge part in the person and the cricketer I have become.

After I had been there for two years, Laurence joined me. Laurence has perfect pitch, which I think I'm right in saying only 0.1 per cent of the world's population have. I read somewhere that it means you are a little mad, which I can relate to in my younger brother! So he came to St Paul's with me while Adrian went to Colchester Royal Grammar, where my mum went on to teach.

Obviously, there were other choir schools, notably at Westminster Abbey and Canterbury, but we always felt we were better than the others and we probably were. That may sound arrogant but I think the majority of the best young singers in the country went to St Paul's.

I think singing like that is something that comes naturally. We had singing lessons but not that many. Perhaps it is something that a lot of young kids could do if they were given the chance and were prepared to do it. Part of my time was spent learning how to read music and play the piano and clarinet. I could both read and play music at a young age but perhaps I didn't put enough effort into the playing because, to me, singing was the thing, and the reason I was there.

To be honest, I have let my music slip in recent years. I just haven't had the time to pursue it as a hobby, but I was curious when I wandered into a music store in Christchurch during England's 2008 tour of New Zealand. My appetite had been whetted, to an extent, by listening to Graeme Swann and Timmy Ambrose talking about music. Swann is a natural front-man who loves music and sings in a band, while Ambrose is a seriously good guitarist. Jimmy Anderson is learning the guitar, too. We have talked at times about the possibility of having an England team band, perhaps fancifully but you never know, and when I was in this store I found myself sitting down at a piano and playing a few Coldplay songs, just by reading the music that was there. It made me think that I should find time in my life for music again.

By the time I was 11 I knew that I didn't want to spend my life in music. I wanted to finish at St Paul's by then, to be honest, because I had already decided that I couldn't get any better than I already was and I wanted to do something different. Cricket! I think that most of the boys I was at school with have gone into music professionally, but that was never going to be for me. For a start, it becomes very tricky from the moment your voice breaks. Your whole voice changes at around 13 – it was later for me – and those brilliant schoolboy singers have to remodel their sound if they are to have any future in music. Aled Jones is a good example of someone who has managed it. I knew I was never going to be in that class, so I made up my mind that it was going to be sport for me – as long as I was good enough.

Laurence is similar. He did what he wanted to do in music and then moved on. He still plays the violin and sings but he, like me, has gone in a different direction in his career. Music is always there in the background, though, and we will probably both go back to it at some point in the future.

My five years at St Paul's certainly made me grow up very quickly. I was mature beyond my years to a large extent. My dad reckons that my time there is the only reason I have got so far in cricket. He reckons it hardened me up and made me prepared to put in the necessary effort required to reach the top. I have always accepted that I am not the most naturally talented cricketer and I knew that I would never achieve what I wanted to do without that hard work. I wasn't the type, for instance, to go on lads holidays when I was 17 or 18. By that time, all I wanted to do was play cricket. I loved it. Even when I was a full-time choirboy, I didn't dream of a career in music. From about the age of 11 or 12, all I wanted to do was play cricket for England.

Amid everything, there was still time for sport at St Paul's. We used to be allowed to play sport on Thursdays and that meant plenty of football and cricket. We would play against other schools, including the choir schools, and I managed to score a hundred against Westminster Abbey.

All the while I was at St Paul's I would play cricket as often as I could. I was playing for London Schools by the time I was 11 and went on tour with them. I scored my first proper hundred for London Schools against Berkshire at Ascot. In my last two years at St Paul's, I would occasionally miss school to go to national age-group camps at Lilleshall so, thinking about it, the people at St Paul's must have known by then that I was moving in a different direction.

I was playing for London because I went to school there but Essex knew where I lived and I had begun to have a bit of a link up with the county, as well as moving from my junior club side at Wickham Bishops to the local Maldon club, a step up to a Premier League outfit. During one summer holiday I played in an Under-12 tournament for London against Essex and met Ravi Bopara for the first time. Even then, I knew I would play for Essex eventually, so I spent more time with the Essex boys than the London ones.

Yet I could not turn my back on music just yet. A music scholarship was how I was able to move on to the next stage of my life.

2

SPORT TAKES OVER

As a choirboy you live a ridiculously sheltered life. At St Paul's, my days consisted of, basically, classical music and, when I was at home, as much sport as I could fit in. So when I moved on to Bedford School, aged 13, I had a lot of catching up to do.

I went to Bedford by chance, really. A friend of mine in the year above me at St Paul's went there and his parents told mine that it was a very good school. Felsted, one of the best schools in Essex and the place where England cricketers Derek Pringle and John Stephenson were educated, was another option, because I wasn't sure I wanted to board, but Bedford was absolutely the right choice and I had a wonderful time there.

Even though, by that stage, I had already decided that my future career lay in sport rather than music, the best way for me to get into Bedford was on a musical scholarship because my parents couldn't afford to send me there. Luckily, what I had learnt at St Paul's was enough to get me in.

It was a brilliant move. I loved Bedford from the start thanks to my boarding house master, Brendan Law and his lovely wife Linda. Not only was he a top man, but he had a dog called Milo. Being a dog lover, that was enough for me to want to board at his house! I made friends with a group of people at an early stage, and we are still close to this day.

It was important that I felt settled because this was a huge move for me. Choirboys often have trouble settling in to a new environment because their formative years are so different from other children's of the same age. The thing that struck me immediately was the sheer size of the place and the number of students who went there. I am pleased to say I immediately felt at home.

There were five of us in my year initially in Brendan's house, all sportsmen, but he somehow managed to squeeze another five in, and we all got on well. We became friendly with another group of around ten people, and I genuinely had the best times of my life between 13 and 18. I can't remember having a bad day.

From having such little freedom at St Paul's, where everything was so regimented, I had hours to play sport and fields to run around in. I played rugby. I'd never been so excited. Suddenly, I was free and the only issue was how to get a balance between music and sport.

I was on a music scholarship but I spent much of my time negotiating because sport was taking over my life. The teachers were incredible in their support. Brendan Law, Jeremy Farrell, the head of cricket, and Andrew Morris, the head of music, were all unbelievable to me. They looked after me very well and we managed to sort out every problem.

Then there was the catching up. Even though I was a music scholar, I knew nothing about modern music, had never even heard of most of the performers, and I had to learn fast. I couldn't even tell you which bands I was listening to in particular but, being the nineties, I guess we would be talking about Oasis and Blur – all very new to this classically trained scholar.

One reason I escaped having a tough time as a former choirboy was because of my talent at sport. It earns you a kind of respect. I was still very small but my stature came from my cricketing ability, and also the ability I began to show in other sports. For instance, rugby was new to me but, with Brendan Law's encouragement, I made it into the Under-14s B side, which I considered to be quite an achievement! I also played a bit of squash and fives, another game new to me.

So, just as between the ages of eight and 13, much of my continuing development was done away from home. Boarding for ten years certainly affects your personality, and it can affect your relationship with your parents. I was taught to be independent from a young age. It's as if you don't really need your parents. That sounds an awful thing to say but, even though we have always had great relationships in our family, perhaps I'm not quite as close to my parents as I might have been. It just means, I guess, that you grow up a little quicker and go through that separation stage a bit earlier.

Don't get me wrong. When I was at home we were never distant or anything like that, and I think that's a credit to the way they brought us up. They gave us such a great start in life without forcing us to cling on to them. They tried to let me find my own feet. If I had a problem to solve, they would try to stay out of it, if possible, and let me solve it myself. But they were always there for us. They would spend hours driving us around to all our various sports and activities. It's a normal parenting thing but you can tend to take it for granted. There were times when all three of us were playing in different teams and they would always make sure we got there with the minimum of fuss. There is definitely an awful lot of my early life evident in the way I play my cricket, that's for sure.

Cricket, increasingly, became what I wanted to do. Being small was not a handicap as far as I was concerned. If you are big as a youngster, you can get away with certain limitations in your technique because your physical strength enables you to hit fours and sixes. But there will come a time when that is not enough and you can get found out. With me, I didn't have the strength to clear the ropes, so I had to concentrate more on learning the various shots and avoiding being dismissed.

By that stage, I had started to be integrated into Essex age-group cricket, but I was only involved with them during school holidays and from the day I arrived at Bedford my huge ambition was to play for the school's first team, even though most of the players in it were four years older than I was, and a lot bigger.

I went to the nets with first teamers and was determined to keep up with them. Physically, it was impossible for me to do so, but I had to try. I was extremely disappointed when Jeremy Farrell selected this other guy, James Degroot, ahead of me for the first game of the season. He was in his final year and had played his way up while I was barely 14,

18

but to me it was a huge setback. I may have been small but I had confidence in my ability and I was certain I could justify a place in the first team, if only I could be given the chance.

It soon came in the most unexpected circumstances. I was having a double physics lesson one day when Jeremy interrupted, came up to me and said, 'Do you want to play for the MCC against the school?' The visiting MCC side had turned up for their annual match against our first team a man short and Jeremy had immediately thought of me as someone who could fill the gap.

Did I want to play? There was no stopping me. I remember running to my boarding house to get my kit, having made my excuses and left my physics lesson, and running straight back to the ground where the game had just started.

The only time nerves hit me was when I was rushing to get my kit. I was thinking, 'Oh my God, I'm going to play, I'm going to play,' but it was all such a rush that I couldn't really worry about what sort of bowling I was going to be facing.

As soon as I arrived, the MCC captain said, 'You're batting at three and you're in,' so there was no time to watch or get my bearings. I was straight out there to face my older schoolmates, of whom I had some experience in the nets. Someone shouted, 'Send him back to nursery school,' but I think that was the only bit of sledging I received from my own school side.

This was my chance to show Jeremy that this was where I should be and I'm delighted to say I took it by scoring a century in what was the biggest game of my life at that stage.

I can't remember too much about that innings except that I reached a hundred by hitting a boundary over midwicket and anyone who knows my game now, or then, will know that I never hit over the top. It was clearly my day, vindication of my belief that I should have been in the first team. I was a very stubborn kid and probably a bit arrogant in my belief in my ability. Then, as now, I never backed down in an argument. I think Jeremy just said, 'Well played,' to me afterwards and I muttered, 'Told you so,' under my breath, as a typical fourteen-year-old would. That's a bit embarrassing to recall, actually, saying an idiotic thing like that, but you learn from mistakes made at that age, and, in retrospect, that self-belief didn't really do me too much harm.

One thing that innings definitely did do for me was earn me a bit of a reputation around the school. I had made a name for myself in my first year and people knew who I was. I was also elevated to the first team and never missed a game after that in four years, breaking all the school run-scoring records in the process.

During that time I worked with three professional coaches at Bedford. Andy Pick was the first-team coach in my first year, then Richard Bates and, for the last three years, Derek Randall, the former England batsman. Derek is probably the most wonderfully eccentric man I have ever met.

The dressing-room environment, with all the banter, was new to me and took some getting used to. Andy Pick, who had spent 20 years in county cricket, was a very funny guy and would take the mickey out of me incessantly.

Later, Derek Randall's enthusiasm was phenomenal. He

would have me on the bowling machine at 8 a.m. twice a week because it was the only time those sessions could be fitted in. One of Derek's great attributes was that he would put just as much effort into any session, whether it was with the first team or the prep school.

It wasn't particularly unusual for a 14-year-old to be in the Bedford first team but I was the only one of my time. The first year did not go particularly well, when I averaged around 30, but I still felt as though it was a lot better for me to be playing in that environment than it would have been scoring lots of runs for the Under-14s. Luckily, my coaches and Jeremy agreed, realizing that I needed to be challenged.

By my second year, I was also the wicketkeeper, mainly because I was small, but I didn't particularly relish playing in that position. I knew I was going to grow, and it meant I had to bat at six rather than open if we fielded first. My priority was always batting and I did not want anything getting in the way of it.

Life was good as my time at Bedford progressed. Maybe I should have devoted more time to music but it was a question of priorities, and there just didn't seem to be enough hours in the day to do everything that I needed to do. I was scoring runs, enjoying my cricket and also enjoying my friends and the social scene that went with them. Jeremy tells me that the records show I played 87 times for the first team, mostly as an opener, and was dismissed 50 times. That's a big percentage of not outs. I also scored something like 4,500 runs for Bedford, including 19 centuries.

One problem that could have had a detrimental effect on

my chances of becoming a professional cricketer, if I had not been careful, was that I wasn't fit enough. I knew I had to do something about it, so I started swimming two mornings a week, on top of everything else. Jeremy Farrell would be in the pool at an early hour and for two manic years I would join him and swim as many lengths as I could before the start of the school day, as well as putting in as much running as I could muster.

I captained Bedford in my last two years at the school, which was my first real leadership experience. We had an extremely flat pitch, so when I won the toss it would usually be a case of bowling first in the hope that we could chase any target down. We had good players and would often dominate.

Things were also beginning to take off away from school. I played in the Bunbury festival for the south of England, which was a fantastic event and one that deserves its enduring place in the cricketing calendar. Then I was selected to play for England in the Under-15 World Cup. Samit Patel, James Hildreth, Tim Bresnan and Tom New, all of whom have gone on to have good professional careers, were in our side, and it was the first time I had been able to wear England kit. It was a lovely feeling, and I took it as an indication that I was on my way to where I wanted to be.

The thing was, I wasn't prolific as a run scorer at this point. To a large extent, I was being picked on potential. That's a fascinating aspect of youth cricket. For important competitions, such as age-group World Cups, do you pick the guy who might be able to score you runs in the here and now, or do you go for the guy who could blossom into a better player and be all the better for the experience of playing against the best young cricketers of that age? In my case, the coaches looked beyond the present and selected me on what they believed I would do in the future, and I will always be grateful for that.

Every new challenge was like a stepping stone. The Under-15 World Cup, played at Eton, was huge but it was always a case of, 'Where can I go from here? How can I get better?' My fitness campaign was an integral part of that, and I had the determination and stubbornness to want to improve.

I think Kevin Pietersen is a bit like that. We are different characters and batsmen but I imagine he was like me as a youngster in knowing what he had to do to get to where he wanted to be. Some of my contemporaries thought I was mad when I went for a run at 7 a.m. in the freezing cold, but I knew it was necessary, and I would try to motivate myself by thinking, for instance, of how many runs I got at the Under-15 World Cup – not as many as I wanted – and my desire to score more. In more recent times, when I have had to go on a run, I have thought of things such as the 2006-07 Ashes series, scoring hundreds and being successful as an opener for England to drive me on.

By the time I was 16, my ties with Essex had strengthened. I was playing for the second team during the school holidays, which was a big thing, particularly as I wasn't scoring enough runs to justify my place alongside older and more experienced players. John Childs, the Essex second-team coach, was great. He continued to select and encourage me, again with the future in mind, and that was a massive indication to me that Essex thought I was good enough. They could easily have picked someone else for short-term gains.

It wasn't all plain sailing, though, and despite my early conviction that I could become a professional, there was a time, playing for the second team at 16 or 17, when I did wonder if I would make it. At school, runs came pretty easily in the last couple of years, but I was finding it difficult to get beyond the twenties playing in the second-team championship, even though I had managed to reach 40 in a couple of one-day games for the seconds.

The key moment came in a game against Surrey at The Oval soon after I had finished school when John Childs said to me, 'You're batting at three.' It seemed to make all the difference because I scored a hundred in both innings, a couple of weeks after I had scored my first century against men for Maldon Cricket Club, and that was the time when I really did think I could become a first-team player for Essex.

Nets with the first team were an amazing experience for a young player. Will Jefferson, who is now at Nottinghamshire, was a mate from an early stage and he would take me along to the nets, where I would spend much of my time observing. It was just very exciting to watch Mark Ilott and Ashley Cowan at close quarters, and see how they did things. Essex were always very good at including young players in their system and bringing them on slowly.

It's interesting to think back on what sort of player I was in those days. Jeremy reminds me that, when facing spin bowling, I was a big sweeper of the ball, a shot I rarely employ at the highest level now. It was simply because of my size. As I was small I really didn't have much option other than to sweep the spinners, because I couldn't find any other place to score. Now, for instance, if there was a gap between extra cover and mid-off and I was facing a slow bowler, I would back myself to go inside out and hit it hard through there for four. If I had tried that as a youngster, the ball would have gone nowhere. I had to use any pace there was on the ball to score.

Derek Randall used to work hard at trying to get me to hit the ball harder. John Childs would want me to concentrate on my basic technique, something I could fall back on when times were hard. And by this time, Graham Gooch had started to emerge as a big figure in my development, a great man-manager as well as coach, and a huge influence on any young player who comes through the Essex system, in whatever role he adopts with the county.

I eventually left school with three A levels in geography, economics and religious education. I wasn't particularly business-minded but I liked the economics teacher, Jim Keefe, and the belief was that if you worked hard with him, you would get an A, which I did. That summed up my personality – if you work hard, you do well, and the harder you work, the luckier you get, that sort of thing. If you put time into revising and learning what you needed to know to get through the exam, you could succeed without showing any real flair for the subject. That was fine for me. Geography and RE I found reasonably easy to learn and I got an A in the former and a C in the latter, which, for the amount of work I did outside sport, wasn't too bad.

I'm afraid I didn't get any qualifications in music whilst at Bedford, which in some ways is a shame. I just played in the school jazz band, mainly saxophone, which I enjoyed, and sang in the choir, so I was still involved but maybe not in the way that was envisaged when I received a music scholarship.

My teachers would probably say now that I could have done more, but they knew my attention was focused on cricket from the moment I first went to Bedford School. I am very grateful to Malcolm Green and Andrew Morris, my music teachers, for their support. They could have made my life much harder, but they didn't. Andrew is a fantastically keen cricket fan anyway, and a MCC member, so has since come a number of times to see me play at Lord's

I always fancied a gap year. All my friends took one and it seemed a great idea to me. After studying and working hard until you are 18, I think it's terrific for a young person to experience something a bit different before going to university. For most of my friends that meant travelling but for me it meant spending three months training and practising with Will Jefferson, a few England age-group camps and the Under-19 World Cup in Bangladesh, which was certainly a life experience.

The first big shock was being made captain. I think Samit Patel was the first choice but for some reason he didn't do it and they offered it to me instead. It was something I hadn't really thought about. Yes, I had been captain at school but this was very different. I would have to be a lot more involved in the team's plans, the bowling changes and everything else that goes with the job.

On top of that, this was a proper tour. I had been away to Barbados with Bedford but this was serious, requiring proper preparation. Representing your country and trying to bring home a World Cup is, in itself, a huge incentive. I was proud to be captain but also nervous. I thought, 'If this all goes wrong, it's my responsibility.' All I could think about was how I would handle the players, my contemporaries. Many of them had played first-class cricket. How was I to bring the best out of them?

One enormous plus point was that Andy Pick, my first coach at Bedford, and John Abrahams, the hugely experienced ECB coach, came with us and took a lot of the captaincy weight off of my shoulders. They just let me lead the team on the field. We were going to be in Bangladesh for a month and I wasn't too keen on getting involved in selection at that stage of my career, so, even though I attended selection meetings, I would stay out of most of the discussions.

It's different if you're the captain of a senior side. By that stage, you have played a lot of cricket and have a lot more ideas about what is right for both the team and yourself. I thought my efforts would be better directed towards trying to get runs for the team than trying to be a young Mike Brearley. I didn't have the experience for that. I was still one of the lads.

Still, I sought the views of two of the best captains in the modern game, Graham Gooch and Keith Fletcher, both of whom I was lucky to have close at hand at Essex. They basically told me to treat people the same as if I was still in the ranks and to worry about what was going on on the field rather than politics off it – and not to rush when I had to make a tactical decision or make a bowling change. Think it through and then go with what you think is right, whatever advice you may receive.

We had a very good squad, including Samit Patel, Ravi Bopara, James Hildreth, Steven Davies, Tim Bresnan, Mark Lawson, Luke Wright and Liam Plunkett, and we had high hopes of winning the competition, but in the end we were knocked out in the semi-finals by the West Indies. We really should have beaten them. We were chasing something like 250 and if we'd had more experience, we would have hung on in there and stuck with our run chase, but as it turned out we fell about 100 short. We had narrowly beaten Pakistan in the previous game, and we all thought that the West Indies were a team we should have been able to beat.

A tough tour was made tougher because we were in a terrible hotel. It hadn't been fully built and the rooms were damp. Staying there was a real test of character. In the absence of a gym, we ended up doing press-ups and sit-ups in the corridor, and for most of us it was the first time we had been overseas for that length of time. Leisure hours were spent playing Tiger Woods golf games on the computer.

I'm not complaining, though. Bangladesh was quite a culture shock but it was very good for us. Those of us who were there know that it will probably be the toughest England tour we will go on in terms of accommodation, and will stand us in good stead in the future.

There is no point in pampering 19-year-old cricketers, however good they are and despite representing England. Players can get above their station that way. If you're an Under-19 player and you swan around as if you've played a hundred Tests for England, you are going to have a problem.

I wasn't a very inventive captain on that trip. I stuck to the basics and was very structured in what I did. I probably lacked a bit of imagination. The only time I can remember bowling a spinner was Samit for the last over against Pakistan when they needed seven to win. We won the game by one run so that came off, but other than that I don't think I did anything that marked me out as a special captain.

Looking back, I probably played it a bit too safe and didn't exert enough authority. I didn't want to strut around handing out rollockings but I could have been a bit more assertive. I was only young and didn't want to cock up spectacularly. We came through early games against Nepal and Uganda, lost narrowly against South Africa and then defeated New Zealand, Zimbabwe and Pakistan to reach the semi-finals. I scored two hundreds and a 90 in the Super Six stage, which was hugely satisfying, particularly as I had slapped the ball to cover against both Uganda and Nepal and hadn't scored many at all against the lesser opponents.

So at least I did some travelling on my gap year! Then it was decision time again. I had scored runs for England at Under-19 level and there was talk of being asked to go to the ECB academy. I also had offers of university places at both Durham and Loughborough to consider.

Mum wanted me to go to university but, as ever, my parents

were very supportive. They just knew that only a small percentage of people made it in professional sport and didn't want me to throw all my eggs into one basket.

In the end, I told my mum I was taking a second gap year and spent the time working on my game at the academy and with club cricket with Australia. I've never actually said I will never go to university. It's just that I always had confidence in myself to make it in cricket. As far as I'm concerned, I'm on my fifth gap year now – and they will probably go on for the rest of my cricket career.

3

MAKING MY WAY

Making the transition from school and age-group to second-team cricket with Essex was a massive jump for me. When I was at school, I tended to be a big fish in a small pond but when you take the initial steps into the professional world, you find yourself a youngster among players of all ages at varying stages of their careers.

In fact, the second team is not really a team at all because you have a different group of players in virtually every game. You are basically playing for yourself and trying to advance your career rather than building up a team ethic. I certainly found it a different world when I started my three-year stint with the twos at the age of 16, travelling to games on the train from home in Wickham Bishops, kitbag slung over my back.

By this time, my physical appearance had changed quite substantially. Basically, I just shot up in height between the ages of 15 and 16, as I always thought I would do. This was the time when I began training much harder, swimming and running, because I knew how important physical strength would be to my chances of progression in the game.

This change in shape inevitably affected my game, but mainly for the better. I found I had more scoring options as a taller batsman. Before then, I had no real power at all and if bowlers didn't feed my strong areas, off my hip and cutting and pulling, I would struggle to score at all.

Now I know I am not exactly the most powerful of players, and I am still, even now, working at improving my ability to hit over the top and play with more strength, but as a teenager this was a significant step forward for me. What it did mean, though, was that the sweep disappeared from my game to a large extent, because I just found it more difficult to play as a taller man.

During one second-team game against Kent, when Joey Grant and Nadeem Malik were bowling on a quick pitch, I thought to myself, 'How can anyone score runs against this type of bowling?' But generally second-team cricket went pretty well and in 2003 I was called into the first team for my debut against the touring Pakistan team. I was 18. The first thing that struck me, oddly enough, was that there were advertising boards around the Chelmsford ground. It was not something I was used to! Nor was receiving a polite round of applause whenever I fielded the ball

A bigger moment was my county championship debut, which came against Nottinghamshire at Chelmsford towards the end of what was a disappointing season for Essex, resulting in relegation to the second division. For me, however, it was a massive development. I played in our last three championship games, after Darren Robinson had suffered a bad groin injury, and scored a half century in each one. That, more than anything, convinced me that I had a future in first-class cricket.

I was made welcome in the Essex dressing room from the start. Graham Gooch was head coach, leading some great players and big personalities, including Andy Flower and Ronnie Irani. It meant a lot to me to open the batting for Essex with Will Jefferson, with whom I had spent so much time in our formative years.

I made my first mark in the field when I took a catch at short leg, Darren Bicknell having clipped the ball straight to me off the bowling of Mohammad Akram. Not only did it settle my nerves, but it also led to my new team-mates telling me I had a job for life in that fielding position! Before then, all I could think of was trying to make sure I didn't mess up. Even when I was throwing the ball from square leg to my captain, Irani, at mid-on, I was thinking, 'Oh my God, it's Ronnie Irani. Make sure you throw it back properly.'

A certain Kevin Pietersen was also playing in that match, for Notts, but he made little impression as we dismissed them for 284, and then it was my turn to have my first bat in first-class cricket. The first ball came from Chris Cairns, it was in my area, and I clipped it off my legs. I was away and I remember thinking that could never be taken away from me. I managed just 13 before being trapped lbw by Charlie Shreck. The second innings was much better and I made an unbeaten 69, putting on a stand with Flower to take us past the winning post. We won by nine wickets.

I have always been one to tick off landmarks in my career and then look for the next challenge. I became nervous in the forties as I approached that first half century, but once I got there, cutting the ball to third man, I again thought that, whatever happened, I could always say that I had made a 50 for Essex.

My second first-class game was against Warwickshire, at Chelmsford, and it ended in defeat and our relegation. As a newcomer, however, I did not feel the pain of going down as much as the players who had been striving all year to avoid the drop.

The biggest thing for me was facing the great Waqar Younis. I had never batted against anyone of his calibre before – not that I had much of a look at him in the first innings, when I was dismissed for a duck by Corey Collymore. In the second, though, after avoiding the ignominy of a pair, I was able to pit myself against the great Pakistani, although, at that stage, he was not bowling particularly quickly. I got to 55 before falling to the spin of Mark Wagh. These days I am very angry if I get out for 50- something because the job is not done, but then I did not have that clinical edge to my play, and a second half century in my second match was very satisfying.

Only when Waqar had the sniff of victory in his nostrils did he really crank up the pace and bowl as he did in his prime. I was a spellbound onlooker as Waqar bowled at the speed of light, reverse swinging the ball with great skill, took five wickets and sent us tumbling to a nine-wicket defeat. It was quite an education merely watching it from the pavilion.

If watching a great player in full flow for the opposition was an education, being in the same side as Andy Flower in the final match was an amazing experience for a young left-hander. Andy, who went on to become the England batting coach, scored an unbeaten double century and I scored 84, my first half-century in the first innings of a match, as we defeated Surrey by eight wickets to finish the season, at least, on a high note.

At that stage, the last thing I was thinking about was playing for England. It was always one step at a time for me, and after featuring in those last three games in 2003, two of them wins, and scoring runs, I thought, 'I've got a chance now. I can make it with Essex.'

There was no chance of me getting carried away by this relative success. My parents have always been very balanced and would congratulate me with a simple, 'Well done,' when things went well, and didn't get too despondent when things went badly. They never showed too much excitement, which I thought was the best way of going about things – not for me the sort of pushy parents that you sometimes associate with young sportspeople. I have always welcomed and needed their support – an open ear, someone to chat to and some-times a shoulder to cry on, but nothing over the top. They have always been quiet pillars of strength for me and my brothers, and that is perfect as far as I'm concerned.

Don't imagine that I treated the twin imposters of triumph and disaster with complete equanimity, though. I used to hate getting out and allowed it to affect me adversely. The deep disappointment I felt inside made me so upset. I also found jealousy a difficult emotion to deal with in my first couple of years in first-class cricket. I was always checking what batsmen of my age and experience were scoring and comparing them to my scores.

When James Hildreth scored runs, for instance, I was happy for him because we were friends and team-mates with England Under-19s, but I was also jealous because it wasn't me. He scored the first first-class hundred of our age group and that upset me because I wanted it to be me. I don't think it's an unusual trait in a sport such as cricket, where so much of the team effort comes down to battles between individuals, but it's not something that I'm proud of feeling. I'm certainly not like that now.

The end of the 2003 season was a heartening time for me. I was still in my first gap year and not yet a contracted professional. My technique was similar to what it is now, the biggest difference being that if someone bowled me a good ball, there was no way I would be able to hit it for four. Now I like to think I could. Yet my game was probably pretty naïve and I was still wet behind the ears, so I had an awful lot to learn when I began working at length with Graham Gooch in the winter of 2003–04. Goochy and I have always got on well because I like to work hard and that appeals to him. At first, it was quite weird. He was my boyhood hero, and here he was throwing balls at me! Will Jefferson and I had one-on-one coaching sessions with Goochie on winter mornings for hours each time.

Goochy is one of those people who likes to nail the basics and he kept drilling those basics into me, over and over again. That two-month period gave me a solid base, which I still rely on today. I didn't know quite where my weaknesses were because they hadn't been exposed, but we drilled and drilled in areas where Goochy must have felt that I needed work, and I would continually hit the same balls to the same places until he felt that I was competent in that area.

Graham's style is to keep things simple. He would talk about batting technique as a whole rather than individual aspects. He has his way of doing things and what he taught me in that period is the basis of what I do now. Since then, he knows my game so well that he can spot if something has slightly changed, and he'll ask me why I have done that. He is an excellent mentor and very good at reminding me of what my game should be, and gently nudging me to make sure I do not get too far away from what got me to the England team in the first place.

I worked with Graham right up until I left for the Under-19 World Cup in Bangladesh, after which I came back feeling perfectly prepared for the 2004 season. I was also the proud possessor of my first professional contract!

It was a two-year deal worth something like £8,000 a year but I felt like a millionaire! I was still living at home, with no real expenses, and it was more money than I had ever earned, or thought about earning, in my life. Most importantly, I felt entitled to call myself a professional cricketer and that was a very nice feeling. Goochy congratulated me but also reminded me that my work was just starting, and I remember hanging on his every word.

I'd never really been found out as a batsman and had given no thought to how I'd got out and which type of deliveries had troubled me. I just hadn't needed to think about my game to any great extent and, even though I knew I was nothing like the finished article, it just hadn't occurred to me that I needed to work at my technique around off-stump, for instance. But I soon discovered that it was not going to be easy to score a half century in every Essex game I played.

The 2004 season was a tough one for me. Essex made me feel like a proper member of the side. Basically, they threw me in at the deep end and, when I struggled to score many runs, kept encouraging me.

I scored my maiden first-class hundred during 2004 but, other than that, I didn't really achieve very much during the entire season. It dawned on me that I had to improve every aspect of my game by 100 per cent. I would watch players scoring hundreds against us and think, 'Jeez, that was good. I'm in a different world now.' The word about players quickly gets around the circuit and word had certainly got round about me. I was out lbw quite a lot in my first full season, the first real examination of my credentials.

I was playing against bowlers who knew what they were doing. That might sound obvious but it was new to me. I kept getting starts, 20 or 30, but couldn't go on, seemingly after doing the hard work. I tried to look at it positively. If I got starts, it meant I could do it, and was good enough at the most difficult part of any innings, the start of it. But good players do so much more than that. They churn out the runs, and that was what I was going to have to do. It wasn't a disastrous season but it wasn't great. The most important thing was that it toughened me up.

Essex left me out of much of the one-day cricket, which was fair enough, but kept on picking me for first-class games, other than when I played in the England Under-19 series against South Africa, which provided me with an escape from my tough first full season.

As for my century, I can't say it was scored in particularly difficult circumstances or when Essex had their backs to the wall. In fact, it was on a Chelmsford wicket so good that Leicestershire scored 510 on it and we replied with 708 for nine declared, but my share of 126 in that 708, Essex's second highest ever score, was priceless to me, a 19-year-old finding his way in the game.

It came in a stand of 265 for the first wicket with Will Jefferson, and that meant an awful lot. The big moment came after I was stuck on 97 at tea. I just sat around and thought, 'I can't miss out now,' so when we went out, I cut the bowling of Claude Henderson past Darren Maddy in the field, who half stopped it, and I just yelled to Jeffo, 'Run three.' The release was amazing. Then Jeffo got a hundred, too, and later in that innings, James Foster made a double hundred. You could say it was a good match for Essex batsmen.

That was another 'they can't take that away from me' moment. I thought, 'At least I've got one first-class century.' One step at a time – that's the only way you can get to where you want to go. There was a simple handshake from Goochy and we moved on from there.

This was in May and it proved to be my only century of the summer, so I have to thank Essex for continuing to back me. We didn't go up that year and they could have easily taken the short-term view and picked someone with more experience than I had. Paul Grayson was still playing then and they could have replaced me with him, even though by that stage his knee was sore and he was coming to the end of his career. I think Paul was disappointed not to be playing, but Essex recognized my potential, took the long-term view, and kept faith with a young player who ended up averaging just under 30 for them.

As far as I was concerned, I was learning all the time with the first team. I had done my bit in the seconds and I didn't think I would learn much more by playing for them again, however many runs I scored in the twos, although I did play for them at times. I was at that stage where I may have been too good for them but not quite good enough for the first team. By continually playing for the firsts, I was able to jump up by the end of the season, rather than staying at a more comfortable level.

It's one of the biggest dilemmas in county cricket. How many young players of promise should play in any team and how long do you carry on playing them at the expense of more experienced players, should they not deliver over a period of time?

I am fully aware that a huge purpose of county cricket is to develop young England players, but the best way of doing that is not always as simplistic as the method that worked with me thanks to the backing of Essex. For instance, it is important that the standards in county cricket are as high as possible, and if you just throw a bunch of youngsters in together, the standard will drop and they will not be challenged to improve to international level.

The key is balance. If everybody was like me, averaging just under 30, standards would suffer. You need that mix of youth and experience to keep standards high. Give players someone alongside them to aspire to, even if those more experienced players have no real chance of being selected for England. Essex took a risk on me, and I like to think it paid off, but I have to be honest and say that, if I had been the coach, I'm not sure I would have done the same thing. I might have picked Paul Grayson as a better bet to score the runs to get us promoted. County coaches and captains are judged by results as well as development and that's why I can't speak highly enough of Graham Gooch and Ronnie Irani for what they did for me in 2004.

This was my first extended look at Ronnie's captaincy methods. He ran the Essex show at that time. He had become Mr Essex. That's his character and that's how it was even though Goochy was still involved. Irani is a great example of a cricketer who made the most of what he was given. He was not the most naturally gifted but he made himself into a Test all-rounder through hard work and determination and, when his chronic knee condition stopped him bowling, he turned himself into a county batsman of the highest class. The man was amazingly prolific in his last three seasons as a specialist batsman, the first of them being 2004, when he was restricted to nine games but still averaged 63. Simply phenomenal!

As a captain, Ronnie was very much an up and at 'em character. Even he would admit that, tactically, he wasn't a genius, but what he would do was get the best out of every player, sometimes by sheer example. Whenever we got into a little scrap, or a member of the opposition chirped at me or Ravi Bopara, who was at a similar stage of his career, Ronnie would be the first one there for us, supporting us. He would never stand by and let any member of his younger generation be bullied. You could always talk to him about a problem, too, because he had been there and done it.

We had a mainly young and promising team, emphasizing that Essex were indeed keen to develop young players. As well as Will Jefferson, who had a very good season, and me, there was James Foster, who had already played Test cricket but was still a young player of promise, and Ravi, who came into the side later that year, mainly in one-day cricket initially. The importance of having experienced players around like that was not only demonstrated by Ronnie and Andy Flower but also by Nasser Hussain, with whom I was fortunate enough to play at the very end of his career.

The relationship wasn't that great between Ronnie and Nasser, so when Nasser spent something like a three-week period with us just before he retired, he ended up spending much of his time with us youngsters. Nasser had captained his country and played nearly 100 Tests, and I was able to watch him at close quarters. We opened the second innings together in his final match for Essex, at Cardiff, when he scored a gutsy hundred and I made 51. That was a pretty special. You cannot measure how valuable it is for a youngster like me to bat with such players such as Hussain, Flower and Irani. You just watch how they go about things and learn.

In Nasser's case, watching him meant watching him fiddle endlessly with his grip and fidgeting with his kit, even in his final game for the county. It was fascinating to see that, after all he had been through and achieved in the game, he still had nerves or habits. He was a great player trying to get everything perfect in order to give himself the best chance to perform. All Nasser said to me was, 'You're going to take my job,' but he was just being nice.

It was important for me to try to work things out for myself. I think I was pretty self-contained, even as a younger player. When you are in the middle, you have to think on your feet and think for yourself, so I saw little point in being over-reliant on other people off the pitch. I wanted to do things my way.

Essex were not a big drinking club by then, certainly not in comparison with the glory days of the seventies and eighties, but there was still a social side to county cricket. It goes with the territory when you spend so much time on the road with the same people. I think I ate out more during that first summer of full-time cricket than I had done in my entire life, and inevitably you end up eating badly at times, having chips more often than you would at home, for instance. But my £8,000 a year didn't go very far, so I couldn't afford to be too extravagant during those nights out with Jeffo, Fozzie, Ravi, Graham Napier and Mark Pettini.

In my 12 county championship games in 2004 I scored 568 runs and averaged 29.89, but I was still only 19 and I had learnt so much just by being around such good players. I was part of the professional scene now, with much to look forward to, but some huge decisions were still to be made before I could settle fully on my career path.

4

MY WINTER AND SUMMER OF CONTENT

At the end of my first gap year, cricket had taken over, or so I thought. But I was to find myself under a lot of pressure, certainly a lot more than I expected, to put my cricket career on hold. And that pressure came from what might be considered an unlikely source.

Graham Gooch told me he thought I should go to university. In fact, he seemed desperate for me to go. So, too, did John Childs, the second-team coach who had been a big influence on me up to that point. I could understand my mum wanting me to go, but when two people who had been integral to my development agreed with her, I had to think about it.

So why would Gooch, a man steeped in Essex cricket, want to take me away from his beloved county for the next three years? Well, simply because he cares; and because Essex are a family club who want to make sure they look after their own and provide the best for them. Over the years, Goochy had seen so many cricketers come in and do reasonably well, only to end up not quite making the grade and, at 23 or 24, being left with nothing to fall back on. They had put all their eggs into the cricketing basket and ended up with no real qualifications. I think that sort of scenario genuinely worried Graham and he took a real interest in the welfare of any young player who came under his tutelage.

Graham wanted me to go to university. 'Charlie' Childs wanted me to go to university. My mum wanted me to go to university. My dad was happy to leave it to me. There was only one thing to do. That was when I told my mum I was taking another gap year.

I think, to be honest, in a strange way, other people's opinions made me more determined not to go. The way I saw it was that, yes, I had had an average year with Essex in 2004, but in 2005 I was going to start as the first-choice opening batsman. We hadn't signed anyone new and I would have a wonderful opportunity to establish myself.

If I had still been playing second-team cricket, it might have been a different matter and I would probably have gone to university, but here was a chance to make an Essex opener's spot my own. It was in my hands. I didn't see any real reason to put off my development as a cricketer for three years. My fear was that I would hand my place to someone else, he would do well and I wouldn't get my place back. When I put this to Goochy, he simply said, 'If you're good enough, you will always play,' but the last thing I wanted was to spend the first half of each summer at university and then return to Essex at the bottom of the pecking order and have to start all over again in the seconds.

I don't think it was a case of Graham judging I wasn't good enough. He just knew how uncertain the game could be and how fickle success is, but I wasn't for turning. I told him, 'Let me take my chance. I don't want to get to twenty-two or twenty-three and not be established.' I wanted to get where I was going quicker than that.

Even so, I never thought I would be picked for England. I wanted to play, don't get me wrong, but I just couldn't see how. England were on a great run with Marcus Trescothick, Andrew Strauss and Michael Vaughan all excelling in the top order, and Ian Bell and Kevin Pietersen coming through. All these boys looked as though they would be around for years and I was thinking, 'How am I going to get in over the next six or seven years?' I never considered I would ever be as good as any of those players, but I did think I could play first-class cricket, and that's what I wanted to do.

At least, even if I didn't make it, I could tell my grand-children that I played for Essex and I was given every chance of getting to the top. I hated the alternative story – I went to university and another bloke came in and took my place.

There is a lad at Essex now in a similar position to the one I was in then. I would tell Tom Westley exactly what Graham said to me. It would be good for him to go to university. But if he is playing regular first-team cricket by the time you read this, I would tell him to do exactly what I did – carry on playing. It's what most of the current England players did if you look at it. Not too many of them went to university. In fact, Monty Panesar and Andrew Strauss are the only two I can think of in the current team. That doesn't mean the others weren't clever enough. It means that cricket is all-consuming these days and you have to devote your life to it if you are going to do the best you can.

On the other hand, all my school friends from Bedford were going to university at this time, and I did get quite envious of them. They all say now it was the best time of their lives. They got their qualifications and they had great fun, so that was something I missed out on. But you have to sacrifice some things in life and for me there was no doubt about which way I had to go.

My route took me to the England academy at Loughborough as a part-time student. Rod Marsh was in charge and I was there with Luke Wright, James Hildreth and Tim Bresnan. It was good. Marsh was very much a 'train hard, play hard' kind of guy and I liked him. He would tell you that black is black and white is white. Rod was tough, but maybe not quite as tough as some of the horror stories you hear about him. He could not understand it if ever anyone was slacking and that's the sort of person, like Graham Gooch, I can relate to. I hate seeing anybody go to the gym and do something half-heartedly. Rod was like that. He would want us to train really hard and then go and have a pint of Guinness if we wanted. It was a good, healthy environment. Yes it was tough, and we would be hard at it from 9 a.m. to 5 p.m., but tough cricketers tend to do well and Rod was determined to bring an end to the perception of the soft English county pro. I liked that.

I don't think too many players from my time at the academy have gone on to have Test careers yet. Maybe that's because then they were picking promising young players for the academy rather than what was, to all intents and purposes, an England second team as they do now. Also, as it was winter, all the training was done indoors, and I'm not sure how beneficial that is. Certainly, by the end of my three-month stint I was very keen to get outside.

While this was going on, I was learning to drive. I'd spend four days in Loughborough and go home on Fridays for a driving lesson. Since that gave me a long weekend, I wasn't going to argue! I really needed to drive because lugging my cricket bags around on trains and buses was getting to be a real pain. It was only laziness, really, that stopped me getting my licence earlier, but there always seemed to be something more important to do. When I eventually passed my test, it made such a difference.

From training on my own I was now part of a structured ECB programme and that meant that my weaknesses, both cricketing and physical, were properly identified. For instance, I was told that I had to improve the strength of my legs. For all my running and swimming, I hadn't done much weight work on my legs. Huge strides have been made in sports science, even since my time at the academy, but to me, at the time, it was all new and very helpful.

Loughborough was the first chapter in a packed winter programme that was integral to my subsequent progress. The other big experiences were spending time playing club cricket in Perth, which I was very keen to do, and then facing spin in India before a surprise call-up to the England A tour of Sri Lanka. Graham Gooch was a key figure in the first two ventures. He sent me to Australia on a scholarship that was funded both by his own money and the fund-raising activities he undertakes for young cricketers. Basically, Graham arranged everything, which was unbelievable. He paid for all the flights and accommodation, and sorted out good cricket for me. He does it all in his own time. It was a sensational experience, possibly the best two months of my life.

One of the great things about it was that we were outside, the one aspect missing in life at Loughborough. In a way, it was my own little university experience, living away from home and fending for myself. I shared a house with two young Hampshire cricketers, Chris Benham and Kevin Latouf, but familiar faces weren't far away. Ravi Bopara, Tim Phillips and Ryan ten Doeschate, all from Essex, were there playing grade cricket.

If anything, the training was harder because it was warm and we could go for runs first thing in the morning without it being dark. Perhaps it wasn't quite as scientific as it was in Loughborough, but Hampshire coach Paul Terry's academy, based there, had everything we needed, and it was good, hands-on stuff. I was in arguably the best place in the world and I was playing good club cricket, although it wasn't quite as good as the Aussies always say it is. They think it's as good as county cricket but it isn't, even though the intensity is high and they hate losing. The Aussies can't seem to have fun when they play cricket. They have to win. The fun comes afterwards and the social scene was great. I like a drink at the right times.

My club was Willerton and I pretty much scored 40 every

time I played for them at the weekends – not a great record but we were training so hard during the week that I knew that even if the runs weren't coming now, with all the hard work coming in, that it would be very beneficial later on. It was worth every second. Every young English cricketer should do it. Most of them do, anyway, and it is so much more organized now, thanks to Graham Gooch and Paul Terry, among others.

The most surprising thing was that I wasn't really sledged. I thought every Pom playing there was verbally abused, and I was quite looking forward to it, to see what it was like, but it just didn't happen. Again, I was fortunate. It was a great club and the people there really looked after me without mollycoddling me. That was fine by me. I was used to being independent because of my time at two boarding schools, and I think it's important that young cricketers have to stand on their own two feet.

After Australia came the Mumbai spin clinic, a venture again funded and organized by Graham Gooch, who does so much for English cricket. Bopara, Phillips, ten Doeschate and I spent ten days facing Indian spinners on turning pitches. That's all we did – bat against spin, have lunch, and bat against spin again. The bowlers delivered good quality spin, too, as you would expect in India, even though they were not bowlers we had heard of or recognized. They were kids, basically, but they were better than any spinners I had faced at that stage and they were delighted to keep on running up and bowling at us for hours on end. It was a fantastic way to practise sweeping or hitting over the top without any fear of messing up, because no one was watching or judging us.

The idea was that if ever we went back to India we would know what it was like there, and even if that didn't happen, it had to help in our playing of spin in English cricket. As it turned out, I was to return to India with the England side just over a year later, and the experience I gained in Mumbai meant that I had a certain amount of knowledge about Indian pitches and what to expect. Again, if you prepare in the right way and look after detail, it is amazing how much you can achieve.

As an opener, I certainly felt more comfortable against pace rather than spin and I think that will always be the case. In England, I hadn't faced too much spin because at the top of the order the bowlers best suited to our conditions are seamers, simple as that. People ask at times why we don't produce more quality spinners but the odds are stacked against them, really, just as they are stacked against English-type seamers on sub-continental wickets. The key is for bowlers to learn new tricks in alien conditions, and I think they get many more opportunities to do that now – just as I was given this perfect opportunity to work on my game plan against spin in India. However, even though I practised the sweep again, it is still not a shot I feel entirely comfortable employing at the highest level. We will see if that changes over the years.

Then, just as we were preparing to go home, I received a totally unexpected call asking me to go to Sri Lanka. To be honest, it was a break I didn't deserve. If you look at my record at the time, there was no way I was among the best 22 batters in the country. I had scored one first-class hundred! I guess they were picking on potential after Kevin Pietersen had been withdrawn because of his success with the full England one-day side in South Africa. I fully understood when I was not selected in the first place, even though I was a part-time student at the academy, and Vikram Solanki, I think, was included ahead of me, but when the call came, I jumped at the chance of going.

We flew to Dubai first and then, when it was time to move on to India, I was ill the whole way through the trip. I thought I had come through my first experience of India without being sick but right at the end it got me and I had the worst plane ride of my life until we got to our practice destination.

Then, in Sri Lanka, we won the first Test and then lost the second one narrowly. I scored 63 opening in the first match, which we won by 197 runs, but the key innings came from Ian Bell, who scored a brilliant 144. The second match was not so good – I scored 27 and 36 and we lost by 39 runs – but the one-day cricket was worse. We were absolutely thrashed. I wasn't there to play one-day matches but, because nobody else was getting any runs, I ended up being selected, and I did okay.

It was a tough tour, though. The heat was unbelievable. I'd never felt anything like it, even in India or Australia. Owais Shah suffered badly – on one occasion he was lying on the floor cramping all over his body and we had to try to hold him down. Even the Sri Lankans were feeling it. It was a heatwave at their hottest time of the year, pushing 45 degrees with incredible humidity. Rod Marsh, meanwhile, seemed to be relishing the whole trip. I think he likes going to the sub-continent because he can find out just how tough a player is in the harshest of conditions.

My most significant memories of Sri Lanka, however, came off the pitch. We were in the country just a couple of months after the tsunami that claimed thousands of lives had struck the island, and Rod made sure we visited Galle, the worst hit area, so we could see at first hand the devastation that the local people had suffered. It certainly put my life into perspective. The train on which so many people had died was still off its tracks, and the outfield at the Galle Stadium was completely flooded and had a boat floating on it. It was a harrowing experience but also an uplifting one because the people were so happy to see us there, and already, only two months on, new houses were being built with some of the money that had been donated to Sri Lanka.

There was a warning of another possible tsunami the night we left Galle and I have never seen so much panic in my life. It never came, thank goodness, but that again was a humbling experience, and I could never have imagined that I would be returning to Galle to play a Test match at that same flooded, ruined stadium less than three years later.

For now, that was my breakthrough winter and it went a long way towards making me the cricketer, and person, I am today. Starting with top-quality indoor practice, it carried on with fantastic outdoor experience in Perth and then featured top-quality spin practice in India before a trip to Sri Lanka that gave me lessons in both cricket and life. I made more progress than at any other similar period in my life. From the start of 2004 to the start of 2005 I had gone from schools cricket to first-class cricket to a winter away and an England A tour. Amazing!

It set me up perfectly for the 2005 season while confirming that I was right not to go to university. I was called up for the MCC side to play champion county Warwickshire and I remember wondering what I had done to deserve to be there, and to have an England A tour under my belt. Quite a lot was coming my way and I hadn't really produced the goods. I thought that people in the game might be looking at me and questioning me. I felt lucky. I felt under pressure. So to score 120 and 97 in that curtain-raiser at Lord's was a huge relief. It gave me momentum and enabled me really to kick on from there.

And kick on I did. The 2005 season went better than I could possibly have imagined, particularly as 2004 was fairly average. The statistics read like this. I scored 1,466 first-class runs that year at over 50, but the innings that really made my name came in a non first-class fixture, against the touring Australians at Chelmsford, when I hit 214 and added 270 for the second wicket with Ravi Bopara. And it came the day after I accepted the award for being chosen as the Cricket Writers' Young Cricketer of the Year.

The MCC match gave me confidence and when I followed that with a century for Essex against Somerset in our second championship match, I was on my way. Okay, quite a lot of players get hundreds at Taunton, but it was against an attack that included Andrew Caddick, Nixon McLean and Charl

Willoughby, so I had to be happy with that. It just carried on from there as my season got better and better, all the hard work paying off as I went from good score to good score.

I even almost won a bet with Andy Flower over who would get to a thousand first-class runs first. I had in excess of a 200-run start on him after the MCC match at Lord's, but he's such a good player that he was quickly on my heels, and I didn't help myself by being dismissed when I was on 999 runs and in the lead in our little race. Andy overtook me but I never did pay up as far as I can remember!

Andy Flower exerted a big influence on me, mainly through his example. He had a tremendous season that year, and one game against Northamptonshire stands out. They scored 552 and then skittled us for 178, forcing us to follow on. Andy and I both got big hundreds to save the game, batting together for something like eight hours. It was the perfect learning experience for me, and well illustrated the role of top-quality overseas players. There could be nothing better for a young left-hander than to share a stand for that length of time with another left-hander who happened to be one of the best batsmen in the world. Andy wasn't an official overseas player because he had an English wife, and he was in an unusual position due to the stand he had taken against the situation in his native Zimbabwe.

The whole question of overseas players in the English game is an interesting and complex one. Counties are often accused of wasting money on filling their teams with official overseas players and those who qualify through having British passports or under the Kolpak ruling, which entitles anyone from a country that has a trade agreement with the EU to play in the UK without restriction. I've changed my mind about this to an extent. Ryan ten Doeschate, a South African with a Dutch passport, joined Essex two months before I did and I told him that I didn't think Kolpak players should be in the English game. He didn't take it too well but my theory was that they would get in the way of the development of home-grown players.

Now I'm not so sure. Now I believe that as long as any Kolpak player is of a sufficiently high standard, and is joining a county at a time when they have a proper vacancy for a decent player, then he can be good for English cricket. In those circumstances, these players are basically helping to keep standards up. There are 18 'first-class' counties and a lot of places to fill. Even if each county has just seven Englishmen, that's still plenty of players. Take out the top 12 who are on central contracts and playing international cricket, and that leaves a void to be filled.

Counties must still ensure there is a clear path for home-grown players, as Essex did with me, but you can't throw too many young players into a team at once because, however promising they are, they're not going to score lots of runs from the word go. Hence the need for good overseas players.

As long as youth development is still properly funded, there is a place for Kolpak players in our game. Certainly Ryan has been an exceptional find for Essex. He's one of the first names on our teamsheet in both one-day and four-day cricket and he's both a brilliant batsman and fielder.

He struggled with his bowling for the first couple of years but he's getting more and more confident in that now, has played international cricket for Holland with considerable success and is becoming a top county player. If he wasn't there and Essex threw in a 17-year-old in his place, there are no guarantees that he would prosper by playing before he was ready. And the inclusion of too many people like that could cause the standard of county cricket to drop.

Actually, when I was playing a lot of county cricket in 2004 and 2005, I thought that the standard was pretty good, especially in the early part of the season when counties had their international players available plus a few Kolpaks and EU players. There were certainly some seriously good attacks to deal with.

The secret, it seems to me, is to find the right overseas players, such as Ryan and Andy, and Andy's brother Grant who has also done so well at Essex. You don't want somebody who converts his salary into rand and goes back home without contributing. We certainly don't want anybody who swears his allegiance to English cricket, stays two years as a Kolpak player, and then goes back home to play international cricket. That's not right.

Andy was not only an absolute master of batting but he also had this ability to make his partner feel just as special. He always called me 'maestro' for some reason, which was quite strange and certainly complimentary for a young upstart. He always made me feel better than I was at the crease. He had ability and confidence and was able to pass that on to his partners, coming down the pitch to make sure you were staying in your 'bubble' or to reassure you if you had played and missed and urging you not to give it away.

Watching him from the sidelines that year was just as educational as batting with him. We used to feel that once he got to 20 he was going to go on and get a hundred, and invariably we were right. Once Andy reached 20 he would take his guard again, and we all got used to his mannerisms and the tempo at which he played, which never changed. We knew he wouldn't get out once he got in the rhythm – to us, there was nothing more inevitable.

Some of the innings Andy played that year, particularly in one-day cricket, basically took the mickey out of the bowlers, especially when the spinners came on. If the opponent bowled to him without a point and a backward point, he would start reverse sweeping, and when the bowler and opposing captain changed the field accordingly, he would start sweeping conventionally. So where can a bowler possibly bowl then? Andy would take any spinner for at least six an over, effortlessly and with the minimum of fuss. He could manipulate bowling like I've never seen before or since. He'd get fielders placed where he wanted them to be placed and eventually the bowlers just didn't know what to do and he could take runs off them with ease.

Up until then, I thought the art of batting was trying to steer the ball through a gap when a bowler bowled at you, but I could see Andy's mind working in a far more involved way than that. He was thinking, 'If I can play some shots over there and get him to move fielders there, then that will open up that area.' I never saw it that way until then, but I guess we have always been different players, even though we are both left-handers. Where I stand upright at the crease, Andy was a manipulator of a cricket ball *par excellence.*

Batting-wise, Essex were awesome that year. Ronnie Irani smashed the ball everywhere, Andy and I both had good seasons and we were a difficult side to dismiss, but we didn't win the championship because we struggled to bowl sides out regularly. We were stronger in one-day cricket, winning the totesport League by 14 points.

The day I will always remember from that season was when I scored a double hundred against Australia. The crowd was the biggest that I had played in front of by miles, and the best moment was when I got off the mark – because I could reassure myself, 'At least I'm not going to get a duck against the Aussies.'

I was probably close to being out lbw early on but after that Ravi Bopara and I kept hitting boundaries. We were playing on the far side of the Chelmsford square, which gave us a short boundary to aim for, but everything seemed to hit the middle of the bat. The only nervous moment I had came when I played and missed on 199. I said to myself, 'Make sure you get this extra run,' and when it came you just couldn't wipe the smile off my face.

The Australian attack consisted of Brett Lee, Jason Gillespie, Shaun Tait, Michael Kasprowicz and Stuart MacGill and I remember hitting a couple of sixes off the leg-spinner when he dropped short. The boundary was so short, though, that they were really chips over midwicket.

It can't have been easy for the Aussies to play a game like

that towards the end of a monumental Ashes series, and obviously they were not up for it in the same way as they were for the decider at The Oval the following week, but it was still a test for me. Australians never really lie down, do they? If they were playing tiddlywinks they'd be competitive, so there was no way they were going to make it easy for us. They were great to me afterwards, though, as Aussies always are off the pitch.

It is sometimes forgotten that Ravi scored a big century in that innings, but he ended up having the perfect weekend because he got hit on the shoulder and wasn't able to field the next day. Andy Flower was the master of that, getting a big hundred and then not being able to field because of some injury or other. We call it ideal cricket!

It was a two-day match and our intention was to bat for the whole of the first day, not giving them anything, which is what we achieved. My only regret was that the game did not count as first-class, but if I was looking for a major stepping stone in my career, this was it. It put me in the limelight just before England won the Ashes, so the timing could not have been better.

The day finished with me getting bad cramp during Geoff Miller's speech at Paul Grayson's benefit dinner, and having to leave the table while the national selector was talking. I hope he didn't think it was a comment on the quality of his speech!

5

AN ENGLAND PLAYER

I ended the 2005 season as a capped Essex player and the proud owner of my own little house. I had moved out of Mum and Dad's place in June, but only five minutes up the road, so domestic help was at hand if needed!

While 2005 was a big year for me, it was a monumental year for cricket. The Ashes series became the biggest event in the country, just as much for those of us playing the game as it was for the thousands of people who were engrossed by it, either at the grounds or on television. Unfortunately, I didn't see too much of the series because I always seemed to be playing while it was taking place, but I was able to watch Kevin Pietersen's innings on the last day at The Oval on television. I was so pleased we didn't have a game that day.

It was just an incredible time for everyone involved in and interested in English cricket. When we were warming up for a game against Middlesex, all the spectators were congregated at one end of the ground, watching the climax of the Edgbaston Test on a television. A huge cheer went up when Michael Kasprowicz was out and England had won, certainly far bigger than anything that was heard during our game later that day! It felt good to be a cricketer, a proud time for the game.

I had been selected to attend the England academy again, this time as a full-time student so, at the end of the season, off I went to Loughborough, now under the guidance of Peter Moores. This was a different type of leadership. Whereas Rod Marsh believed that everyone should do the same things, Peter's style of coaching was to cater more for an individual's needs, and to ensure every young player realized he was responsible for his own career. Peter's regime was far more flexible than Rod's. Your week's work was set down for you and if you completed it, say, by the end of Thursday, you could arrange to do something else on the Friday. It left you more in control of your own destiny, which I think in the long run is better for you.

In an ideal world I would have liked to spend a second spell in club cricket in Perth but there just wasn't time for it. As a full-time student at the academy, I was due to spend eight weeks training and practising indoors at Loughborough – until another twist of fate intervened.

England had just won the Ashes and their batting line-up was both very successful and well established. But in a warm-up match in Lahore, at an early stage of their tour of Pakistan, which followed the Ashes, captain Michael Vaughan hurt his knee. It looked serious but the captain was to stay on for treatment while Marcus Trescothick prepared to captain England in the First Test in Multan.

What had that to do with me? Well, very little, I imagined, until one of the selectors, Geoff Miller, sat me down at Loughborough at the end of a day's training and asked, 'You do know that Vaughany's got a problem with his knee?' As soon as he said that, I knew I would be going to Pakistan, even before Geoff continued, 'We'd like you to go as cover.'

My mind was in turmoil. My first thought was, 'What fitness sessions at Loughborough does this get me out of?' but, more seriously, my head was full of excitement and anticipation. Then I thought, 'I've got to get some throw downs,' so I hurried off to the Loughborough nets where I had the worst throw downs imaginable. I just couldn't hit the ball properly. I don't know why I did that. I would soon have the chance to practise outdoors in a different country, but I guess it was just a little bit of panic because I wanted to be ready as soon as I got there.

England wanted me to leave as soon as possible, so then followed a mad 24 hours. As a young player, you tend to give your mobile phone number to everyone, including local reporters, and as soon as the news became known my phone didn't stop ringing for about four hours. Meanwhile, I had to get everything sorted out, including all my kit and clothes, which meant buying the right kind of shoes among other things. In the end, I had to switch off my phone because it was driving me mad, even though a lot of the calls were coming from friends wishing me well.

Eventually, I boarded a Pakistan International Airways flight and was on my way. Once I was belted in and had a chance to draw breath, I subsided into a state of total shock. This was not what I was expecting from the winter. I had never even seen England play live, let alone thought seriously about playing for them. My only experience of watching international cricket was a Test match between Australia and Pakistan when I was in Perth.

When I arrived, I was taken to the dusty, central city of Multan where the First Test was going to start the very next day. I was obviously not going to play in that one, but Andrew Strauss was due to go home ahead of the Third Test to attend the birth of his child and it was clear to me that, unless Michael Vaughan regained full fitness, I was going to play Test cricket for England on that tour!

My arrival coincided with an England team meeting ahead of the First Test and I was invited to join all these famous players who had just won the Ashes. I was sat at the back, just trying to absorb what was being said, when the coach, Duncan Fletcher, suddenly asked me, 'What about Danish Kaneria? What can you tell us about him?'

I was being asked because Pakistan's leg-spinner was a team-mate at Essex, but how could I tell England's batsmen what he was like and how to play him? I thought, 'I know nothing compared to you boys.' They were trying to compare Danish to Shane Warne but I hadn't faced Shane at that time, so all I could do was give them my judgement on Kaneria. I told the England players that, from what I could see, Danish bowled more googlies than Shane, didn't turn his leg-spinner nearly as much but got more bounce into his deliveries. That was the extent of my contribution, really, and I sat there at the Test the next day thinking, 'Lads, please don't play for a straight ball and get out to Kaneria's leg-spin first thing.' The last thing I wanted to see was Danish turning it big time! Fortunately, he didn't, and the England batsmen played him and the other bowlers really well, but we lost the game because of a bad final day.

The whole thing was a learning experience for me. It was fascinating to see how the England set-up worked behind the scenes and in the preparation as well as on the pitch. Take the manager, Phil Neale. The amount of work he did was extraordinary and ensured that the players didn't have to worry about a single logistical detail. Seeing how Duncan Fletcher worked, along with his assistant Matthew Maynard, was equally eye-opening. Even though I had not been an Essex player for long, I knew that the county scene involved a routine of travel, play, travel again and play again. Here there was much more time for video analysis and the whole organization seemed much more professional with a lot more time for practice and preparation.

To be honest, I batted pretty poorly in the nets during the three weeks I was in Pakistan. In the back of my mind I thought I could well be playing in the Third Test because Vaughan's knee didn't look good, and perhaps that led to nervousness. Shoaib Akhtar was bowling in the Tests at the speed of light and I wasn't sure I was ready to play, certainly after such a long time without match practice.

Even so, I was disappointed when I realized I wouldn't, after all, be playing in the Third Test. You can always tell the day before a game what is going to happen. Fletcher used to give his top six batsmen an hour's practice in the nets and I didn't feature in that. Instead, I faced some throw downs with the last pairings. I guess common sense prevailed in my case because the captain's knee was okay.

Looking back now, I can see it was good that I didn't play. I had been playing indoors at Loughborough and that is so different from batting outside. The best scenario for me was gaining an insight into how England worked and getting to know the top players, and that's exactly what happened, although I can't pretend I wasn't a little jealous when Liam Plunkett made his debut on that tour. He was the first member of our age group to play in a Test match and it made me even more determined to be next.

It was, on the whole, a difficult trip for England, something of a bump and a hangover after the Ashes. We lost the First Test when we should have won it, drew the Second and then got thumped in the Third. More significantly, the group of special cricketers who had won the Ashes began to break up. Simon Jones wasn't on the trip, having been injured during the Fourth Test of the previous summer at Trent Bridge, and Ashley Giles began to suffer from the hip problem that was eventually to end his career. It was the start of the changing of the guard, if you like, and it is incredibly frustrating that, because of injuries, that Ashes-winning team was never able to take the field for England in its entirety again after The Oval. For me and my contemporaries, though, it was a case of trying to carve out a place in the new era.

After coming back from Pakistan, Christmas 2005 was a time of contented reflection for me. Every year of my life up until that point had been bigger than the previous one, and again, it was a case of another little tick. I'd been on a full England tour, even though I hadn't played, and no one could take that away from me.

After Christmas, I was back at Loughborough with the academy, preparing for the England A tour of the West Indies, one of the best places to visit in the cricketing world. It's just so beautiful. We left on Valentine's Day and had a warm-up game in Antigua. I scored a hundred and was thoroughly enjoying my second visit to the Caribbean.

I was very confident going into the first unofficial Test against the West Indies but I got out cheaply, hooking Tino Best and getting caught down the leg side. Then things started to take a very different turn. I was sitting in the pavilion after being dismissed, cursing myself for getting out so easily on a flat wicket, when I started to think that something was not quite right. I couldn't put my finger on it but Peter Moores, our coach, was spending an unusual amount of time on the phone rather than watching the cricket.

It was all very odd until Peter took Jimmy Anderson and me to one side and told us that we were flying to Nagpur to join the senior team on their tour of India, their second trip of the winter. It was happening to me again! I was to replace Michael Vaughan, who was still having knee problems, while Jimmy was called up because of worries over Simon Jones, who was on the India trip but still, sadly, bedevilled by injury problems. We were booked on a British Airways flight leaving that night so we had to leave the game immediately and pack our bags for the long trip to India. As far as we were concerned, that meant packing as quickly as possible and then heading for the beach, because we were going to see less of the beautiful Caribbean beaches than we had been planning to!

So off we went, got ourselves some jet skis and had a good time before we were due to leave. Jimmy and I barely knew each other and had not really exchanged many words, but this turned out to be the start of one of the closest friendships I have within the England team. Actually, it's not totally accurate to say that we had never spoken. We had, in fact, shared some very sharp words during a championship match when Jimmy got me out and hurled some abuse at me on my way off. Now, preparing to join an England tour, I thought it best to clear the air, so I said to Jimmy, 'You know that time you called me a ****, did you mean it?' He said, 'No, no, not at all,' and that broke the ice between us. We weren't sure how to take each other before then but we have been friends through thick and thin ever since.

Jimmy and I are quite similar. I wouldn't say we're shy, necessarily, but both of us are quite quiet with people we don't really know, introverted I guess, but we subsequently found we had a lot in common. That was just as well because we needed something to talk about on our marathon journey. Firstly, we flew from Antigua to London. Jimmy's wife and my girlfriend joined us for a day, and then we were on our way to Mumbai on an overnight flight. We spent six hours in Mumbai before taking a two-hour flight to Nagpur, full of anticipation at what might await us at the end of that journey.

6

THE STUFF OF DREAMS

I remember very clearly the moment I knew I would be playing Test cricket for England, or at least I thought I knew. I was lying on my bed in my London hotel room during that long journey from Antigua to Nagpur when I flicked on Teletext. There was the headline, bold as brass: 'Trescothick to come home.'

It did not take long to work out the maths. Michael Vaughan had come home and now Marcus Trescothick was coming home. That left reserve wicketkeeper Matt Prior as batting back-up for the lads who were certain to start the First Test – and one place to fill.

I thought, 'I'm going to play here.' There was no official word but I couldn't see what else England could do other than throw me in at the deep end. Jimmy Anderson agreed with me, and the situation provided considerable food for thought on the final leg of the journey.

Just a few days earlier, I had been sitting on a beach in Antigua talking with David Parsons, now the performance director at the Loughborough academy. He had actually asked me when I wanted to play for England and I'd replied that I didn't have a time frame. I said I didn't know when I might play but I'd love to any time. I told Dave that my aim was to play well on the A tour in the West Indies and push on without setting myself a target, because that would only lead to disappointment if I didn't get there. I also said that I might never play for England because nothing was certain in life. Until you actually play, you can never expect to play for England. A week later I had scored a Test hundred.

I tried not to think too much about whether I was going to make my debut in Nagpur. The last thing I wanted to do was fill my head with complicated thoughts about what may lie ahead of me. In fact, what lay immediately ahead was quite a contrast to what I had left behind. As I attempted to get used to my hotel room in Nagpur, which was located next to a very noisy lift, I did wonder why on earth I had swapped the West Indies for India, especially as I was feeling ill after such a huge change of environment in such a short time. I soon found out.

Even though, in London, I had managed to convince myself that I would be making my Test debut, I still felt that England might give the nod to Prior. After all, as Matt showed a year or so later when he finally made his Test debut, he is a considerable batsman in his own right, without the added element of his wicketkeeping.

There were two days to go before the start of the Test series when I arrived in India and, after that first night's interrupted sleep, Duncan Fletcher soon put me out of my misery. He told me the news that I never dreamt would come at such an early stage of my career, at the start of the two days of practice ahead of the match. 'You're playing,' said Duncan. Simple as that. He was never a man to mince words.

And I found myself batting first in the nets as a direct replacement for Marcus Trescothick.

Marcus's sudden departure from India had considerably affected the whole of the England camp. There was so much sympathy for him. From what I gathered, he had decided that he had to go home because he was suffering from a stress-related condition. What I did know was that he was probably the most popular member of the England team and an extremely selfless man.

He had been around the England set-up for about six years, had become one of the best batsmen in the world and had captained England in Pakistan when I was first called up as cover during that 2005–06 winter. Everybody felt that he would be around forever, play more than a hundred Tests and become one of the greats of English cricket.

The lads were in shock and it was down to me, an uncapped player, to attempt to fill the great man's shoes. That wasn't the only problem facing England. As well as the departure of both the captain and the vice-captain, there was also the absence of Ashley Giles with a recurrence of his hip problem and a new injury to Simon Jones that was to force him out of the tour. Indeed, our coach later called the week leading up to the Test as the most difficult he had faced in the job, and I can't imagine that he was particularly excited about having me in the side instead of Michael Vaughan or Marcus Trescothick.

I may have only just arrived in India but I soon became aware that nobody was giving us any chance of succeeding in the series. It seemed we had been written off before we had even started. Admittedly, things couldn't have gone much worse for the England tourists but as the First Test drew near, a feeling that we had nothing to run away from began to develop among the lads.

This was the moment when a certain big personality began to come to the fore. Andrew 'Freddie' Flintoff was to captain England in the absence of Vaughan and Trescothick, and it became clear he was going to do it his way – and that way was to rub off on the England side, particularly those of us who were inexperienced and knew nothing different. Fred had so much presence and self-belief. His positive attitude was infectious, particularly for someone like me, who was in awe of him.

Flintoff, remember, had just had the most amazing summer. He had become a superstar, a national hero, on the back of the Ashes 2005 and it is doubtful whether any England cricketer had ever been so popular, even Ian Botham in his pomp. Freddie was unaffected by all the fame. He made the young lads so welcome and, in my case, that meant inviting me into his room for a game of darts with him and Steve Harmison. The pair were very close and had inter-connecting rooms, even though Flintoff, as captain, could in theory have had a much bigger room. I hadn't played darts before but Flintoff and Harmison, two enormous figures in cricket, were very happy to include me in their regular games, which were undertaken to while away the free time in the build-up to the First Test. It certainly helped me relax and made me feel at home among these guys who had performed so superlatively the previous summer.

As the time approached, the aura of Flintoff became increasingly relevant. Fred never felt the need to speak in depth to anyone one on one. He would just give you a reassuring hug at times of pressure, and simply said good luck to me as my Test debut beckoned. The stand-in captain basically said, 'Follow me,' and led by example. That's how I imagine Martin Johnson doing it in rugby. Fred wouldn't expect anyone to do anything he couldn't do himself, and the way he threw himself into anything he did in an England shirt was the perfect example for any young player. If Andrew Flintoff cannot inspire you to try to emulate him, nobody can.

India are one of the most difficult countries to defeat on their home grounds, and the England team who had won the Ashes just a few months earlier were going into the First Test of this three-match series with three debutants in Monty Panesar, Ian Blackwell and me, and had a total of just 211 Tests between the whole team. Our oldest player, Paul Collingwood, was not yet 30.

The last time England fielded three players making their debut together was in Duncan Fletcher's first match in charge, against South Africa in Johannesburg in 1999. That game finished in heavy defeat, but this one was to prove very different.

There was no time to get nervous. On 1 March 2006 Andrew Flintoff won the toss, had no hesitation in choosing to bat first and I padded up. I was 21 years old. When Liam Plunkett received his England cap in Pakistan, I had resolved to be next. Now, as I walked out with Andrew Strauss to open the England innings, I thought, 'This is it. I'm going to play for England.'

I was so pleased we were batting first. I don't think I could have borne a day and a half in the field before playing my debut innings. As it was, I walked out with no real pressure on me because everyone had written us off, and I had just arrived from the other side of the world. There was no weight of expectation on my shoulders and that worked to my advantage. Strauss said good luck to me in his posh accent and away we went.

Irfan Pathan bowled the first over to Strauss as I tried to acclimatize at the other end, and then it was my big moment. Facing me was a colourful character by the name of Sri Sreesanth, who was also making his debut, and he helped me settle by bowling five wide deliveries before attempting to bounce me with the sixth. I pulled it for four and I was away. The thought, 'I've got four runs for England,' flitted through my head and, while the rest of my debut innings is a bit of a blur now, I was delighted to reach 60 before being bowled by what I consider to be a beauty from Pathan. Maybe I should have gone on to score more after a start like that but I was more than happy. My biggest concern was getting a duck on debut, so 60 was much better than that. My technique had proved up to scratch and my temperament had stood the test.

Most importantly, England were competing when we were not expected to. In particular, Paul Collingwood was rising to the challenge. Here was a man who had shone in one-day cricket for England, seizing his chance to prove that he could also thrive in the longer form of the game. Paul had come close to a maiden Test century in Pakistan and I remember him hanging his head when he failed to make it. Now he was the key figure in a rearguard action that produced 149 for the last three wickets. He was left with only Monty for company throughout the nineties, which must have been nerve-wracking for him! In the end, Colly decided the best policy was to hit Harbhajan Singh over the top a couple of times to get to three figures as quickly as possible, and you could see the sheer relief on his face when he got there. I was delighted for him, and wished that at some stage I could feel the same emotions that his hundred had set off in Colly.

We were satisfied with 393 all out. We were in the game with that score. I think if we had been able to get closer to 500 than 400, we would have been in with a real chance of winning the game but we hadn't disgraced ourselves and Paul Collingwood had scored an unbeaten 134.

It got better. I was asked to field at first slip, which was fine by me. I wasn't actually a great catcher but I had fielded there for Essex and my thinking was that I couldn't go far wrong with Geraint Jones on one side of me and Andrew Flintoff on the other.

It certainly proved a fascinating place from which to watch the game unfold, and I could just detect that India were a little in awe of the attack that had proved too much for the Australians the previous summer. Wasim Jaffer and Rahul Dravid started well but India were struggling when we had them at 190 for seven, with Matthew Hoggard bowling particularly well.

The greatest moment of the innings, though, went to

Monty Panesar. While a Test debut is huge for any player, for Monty to make his first appearance for England in India, the land of his parents' birth, after so much talk about his inclusion and whether Duncan Fletcher wanted him in the side, was enormous. On top of that, his first wicket was that of his all-time hero, Sachin Tendulkar – an astonishing start. I had heard Flintoff saying to him, 'Why don't you get Sachin as your first wicket,' and Monty had looked at the stand-in England captain as if he was mad. He had a look on his face as if to say, 'How can I get Sachin Tendulkar out?' Then he did, lbw with one that went straight on.

Now Monty is a quiet person, wouldn't say boo to a goose, but what followed was a spontaneous reaction of pure joy, and since then it erupts almost every time he takes a wicket – an amazing hop, skip and a jump, missing high fives and seemingly totally devoid of all co-ordination. I never tire of seeing it, in common with everyone in English cricket, I imagine. I don't think Monty knew what to do with himself, which added to the attraction of the whole moment. He bowled absolutely beautifully in that innings, and I think we were all aware that a star was born.

We were all so pleased for him. Just meeting Sachin seemed to be huge for Monty and here he was getting him out, and it was a lovely moment afterwards when he asked the great Tendulkar to sign the ball for him. Sachin wrote something along the lines of, 'Well done, Monty, but don't expect to do it again.' He did, though, in the summer of 2007 as Monty became one of the leading spinners in the world.

India were dismissed for 323, Hoggard taking six wickets,

and we had a decent first-innings lead. Matthew always seems to bowl well in the sub-continent. He just nags and nags away, which is perfect for the conditions there. I got to know Hoggy better on this tour, and it was evident straightaway that he was a character who would never give up – a running-through-brick-walls sort of bowler.

India were nine wickets down on the third evening, and when Hoggy dismissed Sreesanth first thing on the fourth morning, it was time for me to bat again. We decided to attack the new ball because Nagpur was supposed to break up for the spinners and it was felt that we would struggle against Harbhajan Singh and Anil Kumble on the fourth day. But I did not find it easy to force the momentum and, luckily, Kevin Pietersen was around at the other end to do just that.

Partnering KP was the easiest thing in the world, even though I didn't know him very well and was in a certain amount of awe. Yet as I was struggling to score, just trying to survive, he took every inch of pressure off me with his rapid 87. Kevin had one big stroke of luck when he seemed to be out, caught and bowled, but it wasn't given, and if anything maybe he was a little bit reckless in not getting to a hundred, but that's the way he plays.

This was my first glimpse of an extraordinary batting talent. I would never have reached a hundred if I had had to force the pace, but thanks to Pietersen I didn't have to. He can just hit balls that no one else can in places that no one else can find. At this stage of my career, I would say I have played with two geniuses and against two. KP and Andy Flower are the special ones who have been on my side while

Ricky Ponting and Brian Lara are the genius opponents I have seen at close quarters.

I think Kevin Pietersen can achieve anything he wants to in this game. Once he gets going there really doesn't seem to be any way to stop him. If Kev carries on playing for another seven or eight years in Test cricket, he will beat whatever record he wants to break.

Andy was a different sort of player but, as I have said earlier, he could play innings that were just unbelievable to me. He manipulated the ball like no one else I have ever seen. Ponting gets the genius tag because he hits the ball so cleanly – never mistimes it, and churns out the runs. I played just one game against Lara and he scored 140 between lunch and tea. Extraordinary. As a left-hander, I just couldn't begin to understand how he could hit balls the way he did. He has scored 501 in a first-class innings and 400 in a Test match. I don't think I could ever do that. All these guys can do things that most other Test batsmen can't do, and that's what makes them geniuses.

I know Sachin Tendulkar is a genius but I have never seen him at his best. His record of over 80 international centuries means he is one of the true greats of the game.

On that momentous day in Nagpur, I couldn't have asked for anyone better than Kevin to partner. He's very encouraging at the crease. He doesn't really talk about cricket or the bowlers, but just tries to keep you going, saying, 'Come on, mate, you're doing a great job, keep on going.'

I suppose I was doing a great job, and the way I kept on going was to tell myself that it was important for me to do so to make sure we didn't collapse. But while I was playing out maidens, Kev just kept on hitting Anil Kumble for six. I was thinking, 'How is he doing that? I can't hit a six. I certainly can't sweep a ball for six.'

No matter. I reached a hundred, on debut, the fourth-youngest Englishman to do so at 21 years and 69 days and the youngest for 68 years. There was even a proposal of marriage from a young girl in the crowd, written on a placard. Thanks, but I think my girlfriend might have something to say about that . . .

It was the most extraordinary feeling. I've never experienced it before or since as a player. I'm sure that being a father, when it comes, will beat that moment. And I'm sure being happy in life will beat that moment. Contentment in life will always beat success in cricket for me, but when Harbhajan dropped that ball short and I reached three figures in a Test match for England, I cannot describe how I felt.

Apparently, Kev was watching at the front of the row of players sitting outside our dressing room and, when I was on 99, organized a quick sweep on how many balls I would face before I got there! I never did find out who won and, frankly, I don't care. I had in many ways been lucky. I was dropped at slip on 93 and had a few other nervous moments, but that didn't matter. It was a case of, 'Oh my God, I've scored a hundred for England.' I couldn't believe I had done it. It still sends shivers down my spine just thinking about it. It's almost like a mirage. Did I actually do that? Did it happen to me? It's hard to think of anything that can ever top it on a cricket field.

Such was the late notice of my call-up to India that there was no chance of my parents getting to Nagpur to see the match, so they had to make do with watching on TV. And, being the very matter of fact, down to earth people they are, they made sure that any excitement from the cricket did not interfere with their everyday lives. I didn't know this at the time but apparently my mum and dad were singing at a concert the night before my innings and had got home late. So, instead of having to get up very early because of the time difference, they taped the Test and watched it as live a few hours later, refusing to take any phone calls or answer any knocks on the door through fear of the occasion being spoiled for them. I tried to ring them afterwards but couldn't get through until they had finally caught up with the game. Then, with typical understatement, I got a, 'Well done,' followed by a, 'You'll never guess what happened in the village . . .' I like that sort of attitude. It helps keep success and failure in perspective, helps me keep my feet on the ground.

I always find it harder to sleep whenever I have scored runs. You just keep going through it in your head over and over again. Failure is hard to deal with in terms of feeling frustrated when you go out to dinner afterwards, the shot you played or the ball you received nagging away at you. But I do tend to put it behind me in those circumstances and at least get a good night's rest. The best batsmen always keep that sense of equilibrium. You can never tell, for instance, if Michael Vaughan has scored a century or a duck by his demeanour after play has ended. He just puts it behind him and gets on with his life, which is a happy knack to have. I

Left My parents, Graham and Elizabeth, pose with me, in a pram, and my older brother Adrian. I don't know where his blond hair comes from!

Below Something's made me smile, aged ten months.

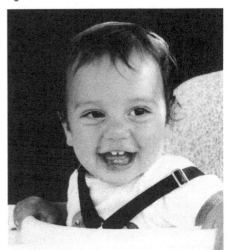

says I can't play big shots? Hitting over the top at the age of two.

We always took the cricket bat on holiday and loved to play on the beach.

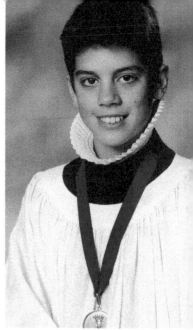

Still a choirboy in 1998, but this is my year at St Paul's Cathedral Choir Sch

Michael Vaughan presents me with a cap during the Bunbury festival. I certainly never imagined that, later, I would open the batting with him for England.

An expansive cover drive is a tempti shot when you're a kid at school, learning the game.

Left My first big experience of captaincy was with the England team at the Under-19 World Cup in Bangladesh.

Below Graham Gooch has been a highly influential figure in my career, as coach and mentor.

ying for Essex against Pakistan, I face my first-ever ball in first-class cricket.

Ronnie Irani became known as Mr Essex when he was our county captain, because of his flamboyant personality.

Duncan Fletcher taught me the forwa press, and so much more about battir as my first England coach.

International cricket can lead to lots of unusual experiences, such as riding a camel in Faisalabad during a tour of Pakistan.

Left The cricket writers chose me as their young player of the year in 2005, and the trophy is presented at their annual dinner in London.

Below Against the Australians at Chelmsford in 2005, I scored a double century, which was a big step towards becoming an England player. Here I am with Adam Gilchrist.

Above The proud moment when I received my England cap from captain Andrew Flintoff, together with fellow debutant Monty Panesar, at Nagpur i 2006.

Left This is the moment of jubilation after reaching a cent on my Test debut in Nagpur, March 2006 the start of an amazi England journey.

s is one of my favouite photographs – walking off with Andrew Flintoff after
ning the Test against Sri Lanka at Edgbaston in 2006.

Right Scoring a Test century against Pakistan at Lord's during my first full summer as an England batsman was an incredible moment for me.

Below I'm immensely proud that my name appears on the famous honours board at Lord's, alongside the great and the good.

Right Ian Bell and Paul Collingwood wonder what's happening as Pakistan fail to come out during the controversial Oval Test in 2006. The tourists' forfeit of the match was later changed by the ICC to a draw.

wish I could be like that, mainly because it makes you less intense the next time you bat after a failure.

For me, the buzz after a good innings makes sleep the last thing on my mind, but that was not a problem for me after Nagpur. I was very happy to go over each and every moment of my innings.

And the big thing I noticed was how happy everyone seemed to be for me. As I've said, I had a bit of a problem with jealousy when I was younger, but I have never been aware of the remotest hint of anything like that from any other member of the England team since I broke into the side.

Duncan Fletcher would always talk about the England players enjoying each other's success and that is truly the case. Of course, you have to have competition in any squad but the key is for everyone to put any individual rivalries to one side for the good of the team. Cricket really is a unique sport in that it is such an individual game played within a team framework, but togetherness is something that struck me as soon as I became involved with the England team, and when I scored a hundred in my first Test it gave me the feeling that I could belong at the highest level.

I know it was only one innings but scoring those runs suggested to me that I could be an England player. I think I said quite a few times that it was as if I had got a monkey off my back, which may have sounded a bit strange for someone who had been around for five minutes but it was the way I felt. As much as anything else, it was showing all those world-class players surrounding me that I could do it, I could play a little bit. I had proved it to myself and I hoped I had proved it to the England team. The bottom line, also, was that England had made much of the running in a drawn First Test that everybody seemed to expect us to lose.

Sadly, the Second Test was much more in tune with the original script. We lost by nine wickets at Mohali and I scored 17 and two. I hit a lovely straight drive for four first ball but that is about the limit of my positive memories from my time at the crease. I guess in a way it was always going to happen. It would have been very difficult to keep on making centuries!

The disappointment for me was that Duncan Fletcher thought that I didn't bat naturally. Maybe, in Nagpur, I just didn't think about the enormity of where I was, and this time Duncan felt I was timid and went into my shell, particularly in the second innings, when I seemed to take forever over my two runs. Maybe I was just suddenly more aware that I was playing for England, and if anything, the hardest part of cricket at the highest level is backing up a good performance with another one.

That was the only thing Duncan had said about my batting. He had not made any technical observations and it got to the stage where I began to think to myself, 'Isn't he going to say anything to me?' It was only later that I realized Duncan took his time before he made any points about anyone's batting. It was part of his style not to rush in with any generalized remarks. His only real comment to me at this stage was, 'I haven't seen enough of you yet to make a judgement. When I have I will.'

Mohali was a massive disappointment to us. We scored 300 batting first, which was never going to be enough on that wicket. Flintoff scored 70 and was again to the fore in taking four wickets as India replied with 338, but we succumbed on 181 in the second innings and were convincingly beaten – make that thrashed.

It was now that Andrew Flintoff really showed what an inspirational leader he is. Everyone felt that we would capitulate and end up losing the series 2–0 but that was not how Fred saw it. He launched a massive rallying cry. 'Well, we're 1–0 down so we have nothing to lose,' was the gist of it. Duncan backed it up with a similar message. If we didn't believe that we could win the Third Test, they said, then nobody would. It was stirring stuff and it was famously to reap the most spectacular dividends.

Unfortunately, I was unable to share in what happened in the final Test in Mumbai. I missed one of the great Tests because I fell ill on the morning of the match. Throughout that trip, we had been eating in the same Italian restaurant whenever we were in Mumbai. We had started eating pizza and everybody seemed to be fine, so I thought I'd carry on eating pizza.

I started feeling a bit unwell after dinner the night before the game, and maybe I should have seen the doctor but I thought I would be okay. Unfortunately not. As soon as I woke up the next day, the morning of the match, I knew I was in trouble. I immediately needed to go to the toilet and felt progressively worse as the morning went on.

I wasn't able to warm up when we got to the ground and

Duncan could see that I was struggling. 'How are you feeling?' he asked. 'Not great,' I replied, because I had to be truthful, and the coach immediately told me I would not be playing. I was devastated, so upset, in fact, that I was in tears. The last thing I wanted was to be ill so soon after breaking into the England team. The whole situation got to me and I had to walk out of the dressing room to try to compose myself. I was gutted.

But, as usual, Fletch got it absolutely spot on. I was in no condition to play. I would probably have let the other lads down if I had attempted to do so. Instead, I had to spend two days in bed. I could barely stand up during those two days, let alone play a cricket match. I wouldn't have been able to bear the heat. Owais Shah, who had also arrived as cover from the A tour in the West Indies, had to come in for me at the last minute for his Test debut and, as it turned out, he did fantastically well.

The whole England team, it seemed, were galvanized by Flintoff's battle cry. We were put into bat and responded with 400, Owais scoring 88 and Andrew Strauss a magnificent 128. On the first day I tried to watch Straussy's progress on the TV but even that was a bit of a struggle, so bad did I feel. There was a huge match on but Flintoff, despite everything he had on his plate, showed what a caring man he is by visiting me on the first night of the match, asking over and over again, 'Are you all right?' He seemed genuinely concerned and disappointed for me that I couldn't play, which was a hell of a gesture by an England captain during a Test match.

I really did miss something special. India were bowled out

for 279, we slipped to 191, but then bowled India out for just 100, Shaun Udal, the veteran off-spinner, taking four for 14, the culmination of all his hard work over 16 years as a highly respected professional. Cue joyous scenes for English cricket. It was the first time an England team had won a Test on Indian soil in 21 years, and in terms of runs, was our most convincing victory in India.

But the 212-run win will be remembered almost as much for what went on off the pitch at lunch on the final day as it is for the dramatic events on it. This was the 'Ring of Fire' Test, that piece of music appearing to spur our team on at a time when India were threatening to hold out for a draw on that final day and victory in the series.

The Johnny Cash song had been given a regular airing throughout the series. Freddie was a fan, and Matthew Hoggard, I think, had it on his iPod. Well, at lunch on the final day I had recovered sufficiently to be at the ground, doing the drinks, and I remember sitting outside the dressing room, with about ten minutes of the interval remaining, and hearing 'Ring of Fire' being played again, but this time everybody started singing along to it. It was one of the most natural things. The lads had been in the field for ages, were feeling the heat and the frustration, and needed a bit of a lift. That came courtesy of everyone suddenly belting out this song in unison, so loudly that the Indians shut their dressing room door so as not to have to listen to the racket.

I have never known something like that to happen so spontaneously. It was almost surreal, and it seemed to have an inspirational effect because our bowlers went out and steamrollered India to win the Test. India were 75 for three at lunch, but 15 overs later they were 100 all out. As well as Shaun's wickets, there was a decisive intervention from Flintoff, and also an early instance of Monty Panesar mania. Poor Monty had a bit of a shocker in failing to get anywhere near a skied chance by Mahendra Singh Dhoni, but three balls later the Indian keeper, incredibly, attempted the same shot and this time Monty clung on to it. It showed huge character, actually, which Monty certainly has in abundance.

Rahul Dravid, the India captain, called the astonishing change of fortune 'a collective lapse of reasoning'. I just called it an amazing experience, as was demonstrated by the sight of Duncan Fletcher leaping into Andrew Flintoff's arms at the end. We enjoyed a night of fantastic celebrations – and there is no truth in the rumour that 'Ring of Fire' was chosen as a comment on the state of my health . . .

There was a one-day series to follow but I was on my way home, barely able to take in what had happened to me. I wouldn't say my life changed, but more people wanted to talk to me and say hello. I got my head down and prepared for the 2006 season, this time as an England player.

7

HOME COMFORTS

I slept for a week when I got home from India. I've never been so tired. That's the biggest difference when you are playing international cricket – the intensity. I was on cloud nine when I got back but when the adrenalin stopped pumping, tiredness kicked in. The whole experience had taken its toll more than I had expected.

I was not entirely sure where I fitted in to the whole England set-up. Yes, I had scored a century on debut, but I had been flown in as a replacement, had missed the dramatic last Test through illness and was acutely aware that Marcus Trescothick would be returning to the England team for the summer Test matches.

There was no doubt in my mind that Marcus fully deserved to come straight back into the side if he was fit, and that meant that one batsman would have to drop out. Maybe it was my negative side coming to the fore again, but, as I'd always been an opener, I was sure it would be me. My attitude was that I would have to keep scoring runs for Essex to stay in the frame and I'm glad I responded in that way, because I've always been aware that you have never really made it in this game.

Nobody within the England hierarchy talked to me at the

end of the India tour either to offer guidance about my career or tell me where I stood in the England side. The ends of tours are never really the right time for that sort of thing, anyway. You don't talk, you kind of look back and enjoy what you have just done. I'd no idea what was going to happen, but I scored some runs, even though Ryan Sidebottom dismissed me twice, for one and 51, when I played for MCC against champion county Nottinghamshire in the curtain-raiser to the season at Lord's. Despite that, I enjoyed some good early season form until I played for England A against Sri Lanka, the first tourists of the summer, the week before the First Test and was dismissed by Chaminda Vaas for a duck. 'See you next week,' Andrew Flintoff said to me. 'Surely not,' I thought to myself. 'He's just being nice.' Then the call came from chairman of selectors David Graveney.

The call was a good one. Graveney told me that not only would I be playing in the First Test at Lord's but that I would be batting at three. Ian Bell was the missing batsman on this occasion. Paradoxically, I had been nervous beforehand because I was convinced I wouldn't be playing, but now those feelings gave way to sheer excitement. This was a massive confidence boost for me. I was going to play in a Test at Lord's, which is just about as big as it can get for any English player.

In the build-up to any Lord's Test, the England side is subject to enormous media scrutiny and this was no different. I was asked time and again what it felt like trying to fill the 'problem' number three position but I certainly never saw myself as a saviour. For me, it was never really an issue. I was just going to bat at three, which was not particularly different from what I was used to as an opener. Actually, I was shielded pretty well from the media. Duncan Fletcher was very good at that. There are certain systems in place to try to ensure that any young player coming into the side is protected and not over-exposed, and I was able to prepare quietly, without too many distractions, for what would be the biggest match of my life.

Lord's is an amazing place to play cricket. When I first played there, for MCC when I was 19, I was completely in awe of the place. Just being there, and even walking through the back of the pavilion on to the outfield, was special. I remember thinking, 'There's no one here at the moment. What will it possibly be like when it's full?' Now I was to find out.

One thing Lord's has is that buzz, a unique atmosphere. It's brilliant – a permanent noise that starts from about 9.30 a.m. and continues until the end of the day's play. There's always a band playing, too, nothing too radical you understand, just nice gentle MCC music. It's a truly beautiful place to play cricket and remains my favourite of any ground in the world.

Now I began to find out what made Duncan Fletcher such a highly rated coach. He started to work with me and show me how I could improve. Initially, Duncan impressed on me the benefits of using one of his favourite techniques, the forward press against spin, a particularly pertinent piece of coaching because we were up against Muttiah Muralitharan, one of the best spinners the world has ever seen.

Before then, I would go back and across and attempt to

play spin conventionally, certainly since I stopped using the sweep as a regular part of my armoury. Duncan taught me to get in a half stride forward just before the ball is released by the bowler, the press, so that you are already halfway to the pitch of the ball and in a position not to lunge at it should you wish to play a defensive shot. It also provides less chance of you offering a bat-pad chance.

In England, you are basically taught to play with your bat and pad together, but Duncan encouraged me to do it his way, and the method suited me down to the ground. Fletch taught me to get my bat in front of my pad, so that if I did play down the wrong line or nick the ball with my bat, there was less chance of it going onto the pad and straight up into the air. Also, this way you are genuinely playing spin more with your bat than your pad, which is not only more positive but gives you more scoring options. To an extent, Fletch let me off from playing spin on the front foot during the Sri Lankan series, but by the time Pakistan arrived later that summer, he told me it was a change I had to make.

Fletch also talked to me about lowering my hands on my bat. I'd always positioned them a bit high on the handle and Fletch thought that this may impede my progress. These were substantial changes, but necessary, particularly with Murali waiting round the corner. Fletch also worked with me on how to pick the great Sri Lankan spinner and I watched Murali closely on video to see if I could see what he was doing with the ball. To be honest, I found it really difficult and I went into the match with a little bit of a panic on over what was ahead of me.

What Murali does so well is create doubt in your mind. Which way is it going to turn? He rarely bowls you a bad ball. The way I tried to pick him was to watch the ball rotate out of his hand to see which way it was going. In truth, I didn't play him very well and if you watch the first couple of balls I faced from Murali at Lord's, I was all over the shop. There was no way I could see what his hands were doing, but Marcus Trescothick, making a welcome return to the England side, said to me, 'The ball doesn't lie.' Basically, what he meant was watch the ball not the hand and you might have a better chance against the master spinner.

I had come to the wicket after an excellent opening stand between Andrew Strauss and Trescothick, whom everybody was delighted to see back, and I could easily have fallen to Murali in those first few deliveries. Once I'd got through the first couple of overs, though, I got used to playing him and things began to feel a little more comfortable.

A big part of that was batting with Tres. He was so nice to me. You could see how much it meant to everybody to have him back after what he had been through the previous winter. In the circumstances, with the pressure he was under and the media scrutiny, to score a century was a fantastic effort. I didn't see him in India and it was none of my business, but I could only imagine how tough it was for him to come back.

I scored 89 in my first home Test innings, which I was very pleased with but disappointed to fall 11 short, and then Kevin Pietersen came in to score an amazing 158. We registered a massive 551 for six declared and were in a great position to push for victory, but then let ourselves down with a total of nine dropped catches in Sri Lanka's two innings after making them follow on.

Our bowlers had done exceptionally well to bowl them out for 192, leaving them 359 behind after lunch on the third day, but we just couldn't shift them second time round, and did not do ourselves any favours in the field. In all, Sri Lanka batted for 199 overs in their second innings to draw that match and it is agony to think back to it now because it cost us the chance to win the series, and you savour any series victory as an England player.

And of those nine dropped catches, six of them in that marathon second innings, I'm afraid I dropped two. It was the first but by no means the last time that the standard of my fielding was called into question, and I could understand some of the comments and was acutely aware of the need to improve.

It seemed to be a bit of a bug that spread through the side. One chance went down and then another and then another to the point where it cost us dear. Sri Lanka had been in no form whatsoever before that match and to let them off the hook, and spend so long in the field, led us to think, 'What have we done here?'

When you get out as a batsman, you're gutted, but are able to go back to the dressing room and sit down out of sight. When you drop a catch, there is nowhere to hide. You feel so bad because you're letting down the bowler and your team. The bowlers are busting a gut and it's the worst feeling in the world when they create a chance and you put it down.

One of my drops at Lord's was quite a hard chance, but the other I really should have taken. All I can say is that Lord's is not a great ground for seeing a catch because of the background, but that was no consolation.

At Essex, I had fielded mostly at first slip but now I had to get used to fielding in other positions, and fast. I think I became a bit of an easy target that summer because of the way I moved. I've always been a bit of an ugly mover but I'd never really seen my running style before, and watching myself on TV for the first time, I couldn't actually believe it was me. It wasn't a pretty sight, and I immediately understood that lack of mobility was affecting my fielding.

I'm always going to be slightly rigid. I'm never going to be a Michael Johnson. It's probably the way I was born, and I guess it didn't help that I was small as a kid and then shot up so much in my late teens, but that was no excuse for putting down chances. Flexibility doesn't improve quickly and, although I've done a lot of work on it, I reckon it will take six or seven years before I'm the finished fielding article. I'm a lot better now but it's still a massive work in progress.

The best way we could hit back was to play well and win the Second Test at Edgbaston, and that is exactly what we did, dismissing Sri Lanka cheaply, for 141, and replying with 295. I was lbw for 23, one of Murali's six victims, after not getting my bat in front of my pad. That emphasized Duncan Fletcher's point about needing to change the way I played spin. I had started to do so but it was clearly not something I was going to master overnight.

However, the innings will not be remembered for my

technique against spin, or even Murali's six wickets, but for another outstanding innings from Kevin Pietersen, which featured one of the most extraordinary shots that any batsman can ever have played in a Test match.

KP had already reached three figures when, to the astonishment of the dressing room, he turned round to a delivery from Murali and smacked it left-handed into the stands for six. You would not really call it a sweep, or even a slog sweep. It was just a unique shot, which made me realize what a natural sportsman he is. I couldn't even hit it that far batting the right way round!

Kevin has a brash exterior but everyone in the side gets on really well with him. He's always been very good to me and one of the things you most notice about him is that he's very keen for other people to learn, not just to learn himself. He's certainly a quick learner and is very aware of his own game. He's very keen to pass on information that might help other people and, even though my batting is nothing like his, he can make suggestions that are helpful to me.

After Sri Lanka were dismissed again, we were left needing just 81 to win, one of those tricky little targets that you know you should reach with ease but often cause the odd wobble or two. Murali got Trescothick out very early and for a while I just had to hang on in there and try to get some runs, any runs, in any way I could.

Murali took another three wickets before we finally got over the line, to finish with ten in the match, but I'm glad to say I wasn't one of them. I was desperate to remain unbeaten, and I scored the winning runs, finishing on 34 not out before walking off with the captain, Andrew Flintoff. It was my first Test win and one I'll always remember. I have this lovely picture of Freddie and me walking off, victorious, and I will always treasure it.

I think everyone expected us to wrap up the series from there but international cricket is never that straightforward and our task in the Third and final Test was not helped by a Trent Bridge surface that was virtually a dust bowl, relished by the opposition's main bowler.

The pitch was, actually, a bit of an issue with the players. When we go to Colombo, we do not expect to play on a green seaming surface, and conversely we do not expect our grounds to have surfaces that suit the opposition. It was noticeable when we went to Old Trafford, later that summer, that we played on a belter of a pitch against Pakistan, perfectly prepared for our fast bowler Steve Harmison. We won convincingly. The principle's the same as when our grounds serve curry for lunch to sub-continental teams. We don't get fish and chips when we go to Sri Lanka. Why play into the opposition's hands?

The end result at Nottingham was that Sri Lanka defeated us by 134 runs to square a series that I think most people expected us to win comfortably. Whatever I thought about the pitch, we were beaten fair and square. The drawn series in India had been fantastic but this one felt like a defeat.

Murali, though, was amazing. It is one thing to have a helpful surface, quite another to make the most of it, which the Sri Lankan did in spectacular fashion. Murali, who had taken 16 for 220 at The Oval in 1998, now took 11 for 132, including eight for 70 in the second innings, the best-ever figures in a Trent Bridge Test. It was not a great match for me. I fell to Lasith Malinga for 24 in the first innings and for five to Murali in the second.

I couldn't help thinking back to Lord's and all those dropped catches. It's hard enough getting 20 wickets in a Test without gifting the opposition, in effect, another nine. It was a big missed opportunity.

But this was my first taste of Test cricket in England and I loved it. The biggest thing that struck me was the size and the enthusiasm of the crowds. I love English Test supporters. The support we get in the longest form of the game compared to any other Test nation is extraordinary, really. I loved the atmosphere they created. It's such an honour to play for England and it made it all the more so to play in front of sell-out crowds virtually all the time. Afterwards, I thought, 'I don't want to go back to Essex after this. I don't want to play in the county championship every week in front of no one.' I loved the buzz. I loved the fact that when you hit the ball and scored runs, you received a round of applause. This is where I wanted to be and it was up to me to prove that I belonged here.

What did surprise me, though, was when I was called up to the one-day squad for the subsequent series against Sri Lanka. I guess Fletch had seen enough of me to think that I could play international cricket, and he must have wanted to keep me there, where I could learn some more. Anyway, he wanted me to stay with the team rather than going back to Essex for three weeks. You learn from being around the best players.

That series turned into a chastening experience for us as Sri Lanka thrashed us 5–0 to inflict upon England their worst ever one-day series defeat. I was called up for the last two matches, but in truth, I was very naïve as a one-day player. Batting with Marcus in those two games was a huge education and it suddenly hit me that I wanted to be as good a batsman as Marcus Trescothick. That remains true to this day. I still want to be as good as Marcus Trescothick because he is one hell of a player and has been hugely missed by England over the last couple of years.

He was able to take bowlers apart in one-day cricket in such a conventional way, and he was so good to partner. Tres was always willing to offer advice and if I'd had a bad over, he would immediately spot it and come down to make sure I was okay. He was so unselfish.

I had reasonable success in those first two one-day games, scoring 39 and 41, the latter in a total of 321 for seven, dominated by a Trescothick hundred. Yet not only was that score not good enough for us to avoid a whitewash, but Sri Lanka reached their target with almost 13 overs to spare. I have never seen such hitting. I think at one stage we were given a bit of a cheer when the Sri Lankan run-rate dipped under ten an over!

This was quite a setback for England's one-day side, and the players were very upset by it, but I guess I didn't really feel the hurt as much as the others, certainly not as much as when I was one of the team that was whitewashed in the Ashes series. That's because I didn't feel an established part of the side. Obviously, I was disappointed, but I'd taken another step forward. I had also seen at close hand how good Marcus Trescothick was, and discovered a desire to emulate him, and I now knew how good Sri Lanka were at one-day cricket. At times they seemed to be playing a different game from us, and that had to be addressed if we wanted to compete with them.

8

HISTORY OF THE WRONG KIND

I had now completed the set for England, having played Test and one-day international cricket. Playing in the one-dayers meant wearing a number on my back and I was happy to be given number 26, the same as for Essex. For some reason I always prefer even numbers. I don't know why. My radio has to be on either eight or ten in volume, never nine or 11 – just a little superstition, I suppose.

We should have beaten Sri Lanka in the Test series, no question, so we had a point to prove when we entertained Pakistan in the second half of the 2006 season. I had averaged in excess of 40 against Sri Lanka and was happy with that, but you are never totally satisfied with what you achieve and I went into the Pakistan series thinking, 'Right, I need to get a century again.' It may seem odd to have been getting a bit anxious about three-figure scores relatively soon after scoring a hundred on debut, but I was very annoyed with myself for getting out 11 short of a century against Sri Lanka at Lord's. I was thinking, 'I've got to do it again. I can't let Nagpur be a one-off.' I talked to Nasser Hussain about it and he emphasized the need to kick on when I had got a start. I had thrown it away at Lord's and I decided I must not do that again.

Firstly, I was selected for England A to take on the tourists at Canterbury and I made an unbeaten 80 in the second innings, so that was a start and it enabled me to have a good look at the Pakistan bowling. Then came the First Test at Lord's, the first under the captaincy of Andrew Strauss, who had stepped up to the job because of injury to Andrew Flintoff.

I was, of course, batting at three at this stage, but the absence of Fred allowed Ian Bell to return to the side at six, and he did so with an unbeaten century in a formidable England total of 528 for nine declared. It was, indeed, the third century of the innings by an England player, following a superb 186 from Paul Collingwood and a slightly less impressive, but hugely important, at least to me, 105 from a certain A.N. Cook!

It was great to be on the Lord's honours board so soon after fearing that I had wasted my big opportunity to join all the greats on that famous wall. At a meeting we'd had before the match, we emphasized the need for as many of us as possible to get on the honours board, and now three of us had done it. But, I have to say, it was one of the worst innings I have ever played.

I was terrible. I was dropped on nought, given not out on 43 when I had nicked it, dropped again off a later caught-and-bowled chance and yet again when I was on 80. I think it is fair to say that I didn't bat particularly well – which is something you could not say about Paul Collingwood. Colly was superb and, as so often in my career so far, he was with me when I reached three figures for England. Everyone has been good to me in the England set-up but Paul Collingwood has become a real friend. I couldn't imagine any England side without Paul in it. He's like the rock in the middle order.

One reason we get on so well together is that we both love batting. I think he enjoys the job even more than I do. Then we both enjoy having a beer at the right times to relax. People say we're different – Colly is the northern lad from a comprehensive school and I'm the southerner from private school – but we are actually pretty similar characters. We're both stubborn, as individuals and in the way we approach batting, trying not to give away our wickets once we are at the crease. It seems to work between us and we've had a lot of partnerships. This one at Lord's against Pakistan was one of the most special, even though I played badly. That really didn't matter to me. I could have been out without scoring, and I could have been out several times throughout my innings, but I found myself on 99 and still almost didn't make it.

I was so desperate to get to three figures that I hit a ball from Shahid Afridi straight to point and called yes. Colly sent me back, thank goodness, because I would definitely not have made it. When I eventually got there, it was a feeling as good as, if not better than, Nagpur because I had proved to myself that I could score a Test century for England without playing well, by grinding out the runs when the going wasn't great. I guess my style has always been more suited to grinding, even though I can dominate more in county cricket, and the reason for that, as much as anything, is the standard of bowling you face in international cricket.

In Pakistan's case that meant bowlers of the calibre of

Mohammad Sami, Umar Gul, Abdul Razzaq and my county colleague Danish Kaneria – and I was determined that Danish would not get me out! There is a picture, actually, of Danish smiling when I got to a hundred, which was nice because, even though he was on the opposition, he was pleased for his county mate.

I managed to avoid getting out to Kaneria at Lord's but that wasn't because I knew his bowling particularly well from my time at Essex. There was an agreement that Essex wouldn't flog Danish's bowling and over-work him, so I hadn't faced him that often in nets. What I did know, from watching Danish at reasonably close quarters, was that he has everything as a wrist spin bowler. He reached 200 Test wickets at just as quick a rate as Shane Warne and he has more variety than the great Australian. He turns his leg-break but if anything he turns his googly more. A very fine bowler, he was going to prove a huge threat to us in the whole series.

Frustratingly enough, I got out to a poor ball from Sami when I resumed my innings on the second day with a century to my name. Once I had ridden my luck, I had a fantastic chance to score another, and this time a really big, century. I was in a no-lose situation in many ways because I already had a hundred, but I gave away my wicket. Colly showed me how I should have played by going on and on while Ian Bell showed what a tremendous player he is by scoring a run-a-ball hundred when he was under pressure on his return to the side.

Did I know I had nicked the ball and should have been out to a catch when I was on 43? Yes. Should I have walked?

I don't think so. That may seem strange to a lot of people but it's a policy that I'm very happy to follow. Fact is, a lot of wrong decisions go against you, as I discovered the following summer against West Indies and India, so when you get one that goes your way, you accept your good fortune and move on. You have to take the rough with the smooth. I like the human element that still exists in cricket, and if you took that away, you would have a lesser game. You just have to accept that if a decision turns out to be palpably wrong, you have to take it on the chin.

Ronnie Irani told me once that to walk when you know you're out provides no guarantees that you are not going to get the odd bad decision from an umpire. So you are down on your percentages before you start if you employ a walking policy. To me, not walking, which is the policy followed by most of today's players, is more honest than a player saying he walks but doing it selectively. He might come across as this honest chap to try to get the umpires on his side but if he changes his mind and stays put when he gets a tiny little nick to the keeper, that makes it even harder for the umpires to do their job. They are there to make decisions so I say let them get on with it and the good and the bad really does even itself out over time. When you touch one and get away with it, you get all sorts of stick from the opposition, but that's the game, isn't it? We dish it out to anyone who gets away with one against us so I expect to be on the end of some verbals if I have been the lucky recipient of an umpiring error. That doesn't bother me in the slightest.

A total of in excess of 500 put us in a very strong position but the wicket got better and better, as Lord's pitches can do, and Pakistan showed that they were going to be a formidable side in this series by replying with 445 of their own. At the centre of it was a magnificent double century from Mohammad Yousuf, who proved to be a thorn in our side all summer.

Yousuf is a truly great player, one of the best. He gets to a hundred seemingly with ease and then the next time you look on the scoreboard he's on 130. Yousuf scores quickly but effortlessly, and he's got that knack that great players have of managing to get away from the strike when the bowler is on top.

A century from Andrew Strauss in our second innings made this a very satisfactory game for our batsmen but it wasn't as straightforward for the bowlers and the match petered out into a draw when we couldn't make sufficient breakthroughs on what was still a very good wicket on the last day. We moved on to Manchester all square.

I like Old Trafford. It is where I have enjoyed most success, along with Lord's, and I think that's because it suits my game. It must suit England's, too, because we have a very good record in Manchester and that's probably because the wicket is hard and fast and has been good to our batsmen and bowlers.

The image I have in my mind after leaving Lord's is of Pakistan practising batting off a marble slab to try to replicate the pace and bounce they would experience in Manchester, but I thought at the time that it might not be the best policy because it made too big an issue of it. The condition of the wicket became an obsession for them.

This was the game in which both Ian Bell and I scored second centuries in successive Tests, Steve Harmison was so good he was almost unplayable in taking 11 wickets in the match and Monty Panesar confirmed his burgeoning reputation with eight wickets. Basically, this was a fabulous Test for England. We won by an innings and 120 runs to take a 1–0 lead in the series. It was also the match that made me feel I fully justified my place in the England side.

My century was a lot more fluent than my previous one, that's for sure, and it came after we had dismissed Pakistan for 119. Harmison was hostility personified in taking six for 19. Perhaps the marble slab was a bit of an own goal, encouraging rather than dispelling apprehension. Certainly we could sense a little bit of fear among the opposition batsmen. Harmy spotted that and was as brutal as at any time in his career, as I could only imagine he had been when he took seven for 12 against the West Indies in Jamaica in 2004.

At a very early stage of the innings, Steve bowled a bouncer at Imran Farhat that flew over his head. The bounce was extraordinary. Another delivery lifted and jagged back at the Pakistan captain, Inzamam-ul-Haq. I wouldn't have wanted to face it, and it had the Pakistani captain coming down and looking quizzically at the pitch. That was such an important moment for us – such a memorable image, seeing the great Inzy looking at the wicket as if it was full of demons. I think it spread doubt throughout their side and made Harmy even more potent.

Steve Harmison was unbelievable. Whenever we practised before a Test, I would look to see who was bowling in my net and hope it wouldn't be Steve. He has the ability to bowl what we call the armpit ball – almost impossible to play and not short enough to pull, especially in an enclosed net. He bowled some absolute jaffas in this game and I was just glad he was on my side and not among the opposition, facing balls like that.

Harmy was another team-mate with whom I got on very well off the pitch. I don't know what it is with me and northerners but Harmy, Paul Collingwood and Jimmy Anderson became close friends.

In this match, when he got everything right, Steve Harmison was as good as any fast bowler in the world, and he gave the England batsmen the chance to set up a win for our country if we could build a big first-innings lead for our side. Setting up a Test win is as big an incentive as you can have as a batsman, and while my previous hundreds had been in draws, this one was far more satisfying. When you are sitting having a beer after a match in which you've scored a hundred and England have won by an innings, there really is no greater feeling in this game.

My only small regret was that, again, I didn't go on to get a really big score. That's been one aspect of my career, as I write this, that I could really improve on. Yet 127 from me and an unbeaten 106 from Ian Bell were enough to get us up to 461 for nine declared and a position where we could really push for victory in the second innings. And we did so, with Harmison taking five wickets and Monty Panesar the other five as Pakistan were bowled out for 222, a truly comprehensive win.

This was also a big match for Monty and it was fascinating to watch him on a responsive pitch at close quarters. Monty never really says much. Off the pitch, he just smiles and on it, he bowls with a fierce desire and competitiveness that has brought him an awful lot of success for England. What particularly impressed me was his control. He has the ability to build up the pressure on batsmen by bowling ball after ball in the same spot and at a pace that is a little bit quicker than most spinners. He achieves that relentless control with his pace, and comes up with some amazing deliveries, too, such as the one he bowled at Younis Khan in the Third Test at Headingley that pitched on middle and shaved the top of off stump.

That was to come later. For now, we had won and won well, and we had done it under the captaincy of Andrew Strauss, who was proving to be a very different captain from Andrew Flintoff but just as accomplished at the helm of the side. Strauss would be the first to admit that he doesn't have the physical presence of Freddie, that ability to lead by sheer example, but he is very astute, aware of what he wants and clear in his thinking. He comes across as a meticulous leader, structured and efficient in what he requires from his side. In short, both of them used their differing strengths very well when they were called upon to captain the England side in the absence of Michael Vaughan, at least until it all went wrong for us in Australia.

I think, with captaincy, you just have to do it in your own way. You can't copy someone. You can learn from different captains as you go along but in the end you have to follow your instincts and do the job the way your character allows you to do it. That's what Freddie did against Sri Lanka and what Straussy went on to do against Pakistan.

And so to Headingley where a win by 167 runs was to give us the series, my first victorious one as an England player. Importantly for England, it was our first series win since the Ashes in 2005, so that was a big step forward for what was becoming a new-look England side.

It wasn't as straightforward as at Old Trafford, although it started off well enough for us. England scored 515 with hundreds from Ian Bell, again, and Kevin Pietersen, but Pakistan responded with 538, which you would have thought would be enough to guarantee stalemate, a high-scoring draw at a ground that had become much more batsman-friendly since its old seam-dominated days.

Crucially, though, Pakistan had collapsed from 447 for three to 538 all out when it looked as though they would put pressure on us with a big lead. We executed four run-outs and took three wickets for four runs in ten balls. Only a last wicket stand of 42 between Shahid Nazir and Danish Kaneria gave Pakistan their narrow lead. They may have had a slight advantage in terms of runs, but the momentum was with us and we scored 345 in good time in the second innings, including a hundred scored from the front by Strauss, to give ourselves a chance of victory. Monty and Saj Mahmood did the rest.

This was a significant step forward for Saj, who had been introduced into the England set-up, it was said, at the behest of Duncan Fletcher, who was impressed by his ability to bowl at 90 miles per hour. Mahmood made light of taunts from some members of the crowd who were suggesting that he should be playing for Pakistan, because of his family heritage, rather than England by taking four for 22 as Pakistan were blown away on the last day inside 48 overs for 155.

By this time Monty Panesar, who took another three wickets in the Pakistan second innings, was becoming a national hero. I heard it said that the one person who was not particularly pleased about his success was Duncan Fletcher. This assumption was based on the fact that Fletch had been perceived as reluctant, initially, to pick Monty because his batting and fielding did not match his bowling ability, but I can honestly say that I'm sure that perception of Duncan's feelings was wrong. The coach was as pleased as anyone when Panesar did well, of course he was. He knew how good a spin bowler Monty was becoming but what Duncan was saying was that we needed batting depth in our tail, in particular a number eight who could score Test runs, and that was why he was so keen to have Ashley Giles in the side when he was fit. That is fully understandable.

No one works harder than Monty on the lesser aspects of his all-round game. He probably has the best work ethic in the entire England set-up. Okay, he may never be as natural a batsman and fielder as he is a bowler, but he has certainly improved immensely at both and continues to do so. Duncan demanded improvement from everyone. That was a big part of his coaching ethic. So I think the media got it wrong if they suggested that he somehow had something against Monty, or didn't want him in the side.

The only trouble with victory at Headingley was that, as it was secured on the last day, we didn't really have a chance to celebrate properly as a side. If you win inside three or four days, you can stay up and enjoy the moment as you should, collectively, but when the win comes so late in the match, invariably you have to move on because there is always another match and another hotel round the corner. I think people sometimes forget that we are away from home as much during the summer as we are during the winter, and on this occasion I had to drive back to Essex because there was now a short break between international commitments before the final Test at The Oval.

There was still time for reflection and contemplation. I took immense satisfaction from having scored two centuries in a winning series for England and I found myself being just as pleased for the other England players who had scored centuries or taken wickets. This was different – no slight feeling of envy, that little something deep down inside when a contemporary did well and I wished it was me. This was a genuine feeling of togetherness and team spirit that I hadn't experienced even at county level.

Obviously, all batsmen would like to score a hundred every time they bat but it doesn't happen. So that means, on the occasions you fail, you must analyse it, consider what you have done wrong, think about how you could avoid making the same mistake next time, if indeed you have made one, and quickly move on to support your colleagues, and take genuine pleasure from their achievements. The team that manages to do that will be successful, believe me, because this most individual of team games relies on a collective purpose.

So the series was won and we moved on to the final Test of the summer, assuming it would be a quiet affair, low-key even, with the series already decided – far from it. Instead, it became one of the most controversial Tests in the history of the game, the first, in 1,814 Tests and 129 years, that had ever been forfeited. It plunged world cricket into crisis.

And it was all my fault. Well, at least that's what I tell people now, and only half-jokingly. My view is that if I hadn't missed an inswinging yorker from Umar Gul on that momentous fourth day of the match at The Oval and been out lbw for 83, perhaps there would not have been suspicions about the condition of the ball, which had suddenly started reverse swinging quite dramatically. Sensationally, the Pakistanis were docked five runs for ball-tampering by umpires Darrell Hair and Billy Doctrove.

Let's go back to the beginning. We had been dismissed for 173 in the first innings of the Fourth Test, a total that was simply not good enough. People wondered whether we had taken our eye off the ball with the series already won, but I honestly don't think it was that. You are always nervous when you walk out to bat for England and I just think our low total was down to good bowling from Mohammad Asif and Umar Gul, who took four wickets each, and some poor shots, rather than any complacency on our part.

When Pakistan replied with 504, a much more common score for The Oval, we were staring down the barrel. We found ourselves batting for a second time by the Saturday of the game, and it became a question of prolonging the innings for as long as possible to try to save the Test.

This time we made a much better fist of it and fought pretty well. I had a slice of luck when I was bowled off a Kaneria no-ball, and I was happy with my fluency in partnership with, firstly, Andrew Strauss and then Kevin Pietersen. Then suddenly, on the fourth day, the ball started reverse swinging. Now reverse swing becomes a problem if the ball starts moving both ways late and at pace, and out of nowhere Gul bowled this unbelievable yorker to me.

Once I'd got to 80 I told myself I had to go on and get to a hundred, because you feel you have done the hard work by getting that far. So I was gutted when I was given out. The first thing you do when you get back to the dressing room is check the replays and I soon saw that I could have no complaints about the decision. I was definitely out.

Then KP started hitting it around before getting out for 96. After I emerged from the shower and started to watch the game again, I became aware that Darrell had penalized them five runs. I thought that was quite funny, but someone, I think it was Duncan Fletcher, soon said, 'No, this is serious. They've been accused of ball-tampering,' and we turned the sound up on the TV to listen to what the commentators were saying about it.

It was very clear that this was a serious allegation and there was a sort of nervous excitement in the England dressing room. Certainly, I found it all very exciting. I was so raw and naïve, looking back. Paul Collingwood and Ian Bell were at the crease when the players came off for tea on that Sunday and confirmed to us that Darrell had told them the ball had been changed because its condition had been altered.

Next thing we knew the door had been firmly shut on the Pakistani dressing room, our batsmen had returned to resume the match but there was no sign of the opposition. They weren't coming back. They had been accused of something very serious that they didn't believe they had done and they were protesting by not resuming play. This really was amazing and I could not believe it was happening.

The umpires took the bails off and declared the match over, and the whole thing became a massive farce, particularly when Pakistan subsequently came out of their dressing room to begin again only to be told by the umpires that they were too late and the match was over. I was pleased that I was there to witness this drama being played out, to be a part of it, so I could tell people about it in 20 or 30 years' time.

It took quite a while to settle down. We weren't allowed out of our dressing room in case tensions were running high, but when we did emerge we still weren't quite sure what was going on. As far as the umpires were concerned, the game was over, but nobody seemed totally sure whether that was it or whether some sort of agreement would be reached to enable us to resume play the next day.

As a team, we couldn't see how the game could carry on because surely you couldn't just miss a session and then start again. We went back to our hotel to be greeted by a strong media presence and were told to say nothing. It was like being at the centre of a storm, one that I quickly realized was dominating every news broadcast.

We were convinced the match was over, so we sat in the hotel bar that night, had a couple of drinks and watched the news coverage on the TV. At 9 p.m. we were told that the game was definitely over. Pakistan had forfeited and we had won the match and the series 3–0 – from a position where we might well have lost, too.

At no point did we have any discussions with the Pakistani players, because I think they had been told to stick together. There had been no trouble between the teams throughout the series. It had been played in the right spirit and the last thing we expected was something like this to explode on us. The next day we drove to the ground to collect our kit and that was it. Well, that was it for us, but the repercussions went on and on.

Darrell Hair, whom I had found, in my limited experience, to be a fair umpire and a nice person to talk to, was accused of a heavy-handed approach on the field and intransigence off it. Apparently, no culprit had been identified by the television pictures so no one individual was ever actually accused of tampering with the ball and the whole team had taken collective blame.

The consequences of the whole affair were enormous. Hair faced a number of accusations and resigned from his umpiring job with the ICC. Inzamam-ul-Haq was charged with bringing the game into disrepute and there was talk of Pakistan refusing to take part in the forthcoming one-day series if their captain was banned. In the end, the one-day show went on, Hair was out of the game for 18 months before returning to officiate in the Second Test of the 2008 summer between England and New Zealand at Old Trafford, and much of our good cricket that summer had been overshadowed.

We never got to pick up the trophy for winning the series, which I deeply regret. To pick up trophies like that is the best bit about playing Test cricket, it's why you do it, to try to win and relish the moment of victory. It took the shine off the whole achievement.

Yet it had been a momentous summer for England and for me, from arriving in India as a replacement and scoring a century on debut to becoming established in the England side with more centuries and a series success against a world-class side in the shape of Pakistan. What lay ahead was even more momentous – an Ashes series in Australia, with England going there as holders. It doesn't get any bigger than that.

9

THE BATTLE FOR THE ASHES

I was not involved in the one-day series that finished the 2006 season, so I heeded the advice of Duncan Fletcher that we should get ourselves as fit as we possibly could before what would be the biggest series that any of us had ever played up until that point – England's defence of the Ashes.

I trained as hard as I have ever done for about a month, and tried not to take any notice of the media hype that was already starting to build around the series. The interest was inevitable. After all, English cricket had never seen such scenes as greeted our team's incredible victory in 2005, and this was to be the defence of the biggest prize in cricket on Australian soil. But I didn't want to psych myself out by building it up too much in my mind. 'It's the Ashes. It's Australia. It's huge,' was not what I wanted to be thinking to myself. The key, at least at that stage, was to try to treat it like any other series, but whether I achieved that or not I'm not sure.

Even when the side was announced and I knew I would be part of this massive event, I tried not to think too much about it. I knew how draining it would be mentally when we got there, and there were already lots of reports about how hard it is to play in Australia and how both the media and the crowds would get on our backs at every opportunity. The last thing I wanted to do was to make that worse.

As it turned out, we kind of slipped into the country and had five or six fairly anonymous days before we were thrashed in a warm-up game, a one-day match, which I found a bit odd as we were preparing to play five Tests for the Ashes. I wasn't too concerned about our defeat because we were preparing for the long game, but I can't ever remember getting so much stick from a crowd in any cricket match in my life. I thought, 'If this is what it's going to be like, we're in for a rough ride . . .'

What really struck me about the verbal abuse was the lack of humour involved. If English crowds hand out stick, there is invariably a light-hearted feel about it, some clever comments and a nice atmosphere. This was just dour. The people at Canberra that day never seemed to tire of saying the same offensive things about my mum, or whatever they found amusing at the time. The next day in one of the local papers there was a big picture of Ashley Giles walking off the pitch after he'd been dismissed, with a headline that blasted 'How did we lose the Ashes to this lot?' I thought, 'Here we go . . .'

The thing is, it never actually gets to you. You just shrug it off because although a barrage comes at you, you can't say anything back because you're on a hiding to nothing. It did make me wonder what it was going to be like when the Tests started but in Canberra the spectators were all Australian and by the time of the First Test, the Barmy Army had arrived to even things up.

Another thing that struck me was that the Australian media seemed to be totally behind their team, as if they were cheerleaders, all helping the team to get the little urn back. It was in stark contrast to our media, where criticism of the England team is quite commonplace. I am not saying one is right and one is wrong, it was just striking how different the two attitudes were.

Sadly, Marcus Trescothick had to go home again before the big matches had even started. Everybody felt desperately sorry for such a popular man. I still didn't know Marcus that well. He had seemed fine. The story in those early stages of the tour was, 'Which batsman is going to miss out on an Ashes place, Cook, Bell or Collingwood?' I wasn't sure at all if I was going to be in the First Test team but one thing seemed certain – Tres would be. Now, without the team even knowing something was wrong, we came off the field during the warm-up game in Sydney and Marcus wasn't there. He had gone before we knew what had happened or had the chance to say goodbye.

I think Marcus preferred it that way. I can't imagine he would have wanted a big scene. It was just so terribly sad and a setback for the England team because he was and is such a formidable player. We needed him on that tour, that's for sure. His experience was missed terribly and Tres's departure put a real dampener on the start of the tour after we had gone there so full of confidence. Suddenly to discover that he had gone really affected people, I think. As it turned out, there weren't many good days on that tour, but that definitely set the tone.

The thing is, cricket really does become secondary at times like that. Everybody felt so sorry for Tres and could only imagine what he was going through. I can honestly say I wasn't thinking about the implications for me at the time but it did soon dawn on me that the chances were I would be playing now. I had been going in at three but this meant that I would probably be batting in the biggest cricket series of all time as an opener, right up there in the eye of any storm that was going to come our way. It was nerve-wracking, but also enormously exciting.

I had my first taste back at the top of the order in the first-class warm-up game against South Australia in Adelaide, which passed reasonably uneventfully. The thing I most had to get used to was batting against the Kookaburra ball, which stopped swinging much quicker than the Dukes ball used in England – that and being under siege from the Australian media. It had almost got amusing by now, even though the real business had yet to begin.

When the big day arrived, we were nervous but, I would contend, no different from the Australians. They had been under pressure for 18 months to get the Ashes back and it seemed as though nobody in that vast country was prepared to let them fail for a second time.

There had been no big team meeting for us. No one needed motivation for a contest such as this. We were just trying to keep our heads as cool and as clear as we could. We had to try to stay with the Aussies for as long as possible, so their media might turn on them.

It has been said that we were unusually quiet on the bus on the way to the Gabba in Brisbane for that first day, but, to be honest, it's always quiet on the bus going to a match. I've never been on a team bus at the beginning of any Test series when it has been really loud. Everyone is usually concentrating on what lies ahead of them, often listening to music on their iPods. The atmosphere on the way back at the end of a day's play is usually much more animated. So yes, the first day at Brisbane was quiet, but I really wouldn't read too much into that.

Likewise, too much should not be read into the impact the first ball of the Ashes series had on us. It has gone down as a highly significant moment but we can hardly blame what became an Ashes thrashing on Steve Harmison's first ball.

I cannot ever remember an atmosphere quite like the one that greeted us before that first ball after we had lost the toss and been asked to field. I was at short leg wearing a helmet and the noise was immense before Harmy let that first ball slip and fly towards Andrew Flintoff, our captain in the continued absence of Michael Vaughan, at second slip to be signalled wide by umpire Steve Bucknor. But one ball doesn't lose you a Test series.

Steve was under the cosh and clearly nervous. Only he knows what happened but the memory of it followed him around for the rest of the series, with the most vociferous supporters targeting him for abuse. Yet what has since been overlooked is that the Aussies were very nervous as well. I'm convinced of that. Just watch that first hour again on DVD, if you can. The way Justin Langer played through gully and third man was evidence of it. But the key was that the Aussies fought their way through it, and they deserve immense credit for that.

In truth, once they got through that hour or so of nerves, Australia never looked back. They gained more and more momentum as the first day and the game went on, and the horse had bolted before we seemed to have much of a chance to catch it.

By the end of the first day of the most eagerly awaited Ashes series in history, Australia were 346 for three and we were up against it. By the close of the second, the hosts had racked up 602 for nine declared and taken our first three wickets, including me for 11, caught Shane Warne bowled Glenn McGrath, two of the most famous figures in Australian cricket history, in my debut Ashes innings.

To try to take our minds off of what was unfolding, at the end of the second day the team went, *en masse*, to see the Borat film, which was popular at the time. I remember just sitting there and laughing throughout the whole movie. It was, in effect, an antidote. For just a short while, we were able to forget our troubles and relax, but the mood did not stay light-hearted for nearly long enough. The First Test went from bad to worse as we were rolled over for 157 with McGrath taking six wickets. Then, after Australia had rattled along to 202 for one in their second innings, we were dismissed a second time for a much better 370, including a contribution of 43 from me.

In situations like that, all you can do is try to take as many positives as you can. We were a lot better in the second innings. Paul Collingwood and Kevin Pietersen came close to scoring centuries. We showed a lot more fight. But the bottom line is that we were thoroughly beaten and, realistically, the way we played in the second innings was irrelevant. We were well beaten by then.

Somehow, we had to put it behind us and prepare for the Second Test in Adelaide. We had to forget what had happened and start again. And you have to say that for four days of that Second Test we competed superbly well – so well that it really did seem as though we were back in with a real shout of making an impact in this Ashes series, and Brisbane could be consigned to history as something of a bad dream. Scoring 551 for six declared should make defeat impossible. We won the toss and compiled an innings that conjured up memories of 2005 and how well that had gone. At the centre of it was the man whom the Australians had ribbed mercilessly for his supporting role in England winning the Ashes, Paul Collingwood.

Paul had played in just one of that series, the famous last Test at The Oval, as a replacement for the injured Simon Jones, but now, as an established member of England's Test side, he enjoyed his greatest hour. Colly was simply magnificent in the first innings of that Second Test in Adelaide. People talk about him being a gritty player and there was certainly plenty of grit in his innings that day, but there was so much more. His 206 was fluid and quite brilliant. Not only that, it was the first Test double century by an England player in Australia since Wally Hammond 70 years earlier. When you think how many great players there had been since then, that is a truly awesome achievement.

Once Paul settles in at the crease, he aims for a big score, and this was probably the best innings he had ever played in his life. It was accomplished mainly in partnership with Pietersen, who scored 158 – amazingly, the third time he had made that score in his first 20 Tests, including on the last day at The Oval when England secured the Ashes. An omen perhaps?

The character showed by those two put us right back in the series, and when we took three quick Aussie wickets, we could start to dream. Much has subsequently been made of

Ashley Giles dropping Ricky Ponting, a miss that turned out to be highly expensive because the Australian captain went on to score 142, but we all drop catches. As ever, it was far too simplistic to lay the blame at Ashley's door.

Matthew Hoggard bowled magnificently to take seven wickets but Australia managed to reach 513 on the fourth day and, to all intents and purposes, it looked as though the match would be drawn and we would head to Perth for the Third Test still one down. When your team can boast individual performances of the calibre of Collingwood's, Pietersen's and Hoggard's in the same match, you would think that you were at least safe and possibly in a position of dominance.

But no. From something like 200 behind at the end of the third day, Australia managed to grind their way somewhere close to parity, and then they dismissed me cheaply before the close of the penultimate day. Still the draw was the massive favourite but we all knew about the perils of fifth-day cricket. It is why Test cricket remains the greatest game. Things can change, and change they did.

I have never seen anything like the fifth day of the Second Test. All we had in our sights was batting out for the draw. A lot of credit must go to the bowlers, Warne in particular. Maybe we retreated too much into our shells. Maybe we weren't positive enough in building a lead that would have proved impossible for Australia to reach in the time left. It is very hard balancing attack and defence when trying to bat time to save a game.

From 69 for one on that last day, we fell to 129 all out, leaving Australia needing 168 to win in 36 overs, and all the while I could do nothing other than sit there in a state of helplessness. I was helpless when Andrew Strauss fell victim to a questionable catch and helpless when Ian Bell was run out. We were all helpless as Shane Warne took a grip and we fell under his spell. A quick 40 or 50 from one of our batsmen would have made it safe for us, but it was beyond all of us. Australia's target was far from straightforward. Yet they did it with 19 balls to spare.

The England dressing room that night was the worst I have known. Being beaten in Brisbane was bad. This was so much worse. Nobody could say a word. We were all trying to understand what on earth had happened. It was unbelievable. The Ashes that had been so hard to win were slipping from our grasp just two matches after the start of the series.

But you never believe that something has gone until there is nothing left for you to do. We knew we had to produce a magic recovery, and in sport anything's possible. We had to believe we could still do it but I think, deep down, we all knew it would be a monumental achievement from there.

Meanwhile, the Australians were celebrating as if they had already recovered the urn. To be fair, it was an amazing victory on their part. They hung on in there, as they do, and then pounced when they had an opportunity to show what a good side they are. You can usually hear the opposition celebrating after you are beaten and this time the noise was as great as you are likely to hear.

By this time, I had been given a pretty good idea of what it was like to play against Australia. Their bowlers were relentless, executing their plans with amazing precision and determination, but relentlessness is nothing without skill. It was quite clear that they were targeting my off-stump and they never gave me anything to cut or short enough to leave. I hadn't got many runs, we were 2–0 down and I was worried about my form. It was the most testing of circumstances.

But it was soon put into perspective by the news that Ashley Giles had to go home because his wife had been taken very ill. It was horrible news for a really good man, who didn't deserve to be carrying so much of the blame for what happened to us in Adelaide because he had dropped Ricky Ponting.

There was also, of course, the matter of whether Ashley should have been playing in the first place. The decision to prefer him to Monty Panesar as our spinner had become a controversial issue. With hindsight, it was probably the wrong decision but that is no disrespect to Ashley. Duncan Fletcher had preferred him to Monty because Ashley offers so much more to the team in terms of his batting, and the fact that he was an Ashes winner and an excellent team man, but Monty proved that he should have played from the start by taking eight wickets in the Third Test in Perth, the match in which we lost the Ashes.

We were well in the game when we dismissed Australia for 244, with Panesar taking five wickets, but again we didn't score enough runs in the first innings. To be bowled out ourselves for 215 was a real wasted opportunity and one from which we were not able to recover. At the halfway mark of the game we still fancied our chances, but the Test and the Ashes were taken away from us in spectacular fashion by one of the quickest and greatest centuries of all time.

Adam Gilchrist is an amazing batsman but even he had never produced anything to match that innings in Perth. I was fielding at midwicket when he started and I remember the ball going farther and farther back, and as more sixes flew over my head, the crowd were whipped up and the stick we all received while fielding on the boundary intensified.

Gilchrist hadn't scored many runs up until then but that's what great players and great sides do, deliver when it matters. It was a one-day innings, really, but it was a match-winning innings and I guess I can say now that it was an honour to be there, even though it didn't feel that way at the time. When you are so deeply committed to winning, you don't appreciate what you are a part of, but there are things that you will tell your children and grandchildren and, in my case, I'll be saying that I played against some true greats in Shane Warne, Glenn McGrath and Adam Gilchrist before they retired. I just won't tell the grandchildren what the result was!

And I will tell them that another left-hander scored a century in the same match as Gilchrist! I felt at home in Perth, having spent some time there. I was convinced I would score runs at the WACA and I duly scored my first Ashes hundred in the second innings. We were trying to bat out for a draw, which, unfortunately, we were not able to do, but that century did prove to me that I could do it in Australia. I'd averaged around 30 in the series up to that point, and although in the wider scheme of things those runs didn't mean too much, they did mean an awful lot to me. They meant I could play against the very best.

The Australian players were brilliant to me. Obviously, a few beers were downed after the game because they had won the Ashes, but they took the time to say well played to me. On the field they play very tough, but off it they always go about the game in the right way.

It was the only nice part about the aftermath of the Third Test. We just had to sit there and watch the Australian celebrations, seeing our worst nightmare become reality. It was a horrible feeling to have lost so quickly. The Ashes had taken so long to win. We had been absolutely thrashed.

Christmas in Melbourne was accompanied by some unseasonal snow, and the ECB put on a great spread for our families. The mood would have been a lot better had we been three up rather than three down, of course, but the kids enjoyed themselves just as much, which was heartening.

Our big motivating factor now was to try to avoid a 5–0 whitewash, which had only ever happened once before. Freddie Flintoff didn't want to be the captain who lost 5–0 and we didn't want to be the team to do it, either. However, Australia had gained a momentum that we just couldn't stop. It was like a snowball effect where everything that could go wrong for us did so. Warne went to 700 Test wickets and said he would retire at the end of the series. McGrath and Justin Langer followed him. It had all gone for us. I'm not sure whether embarrassment is the right word to sum up my feelings at the end, but I know it was the worst I had ever felt about anything.

Later came the time for reflection and trying to learn from the whole experience. I never like to analyse my dismissals while a series is going on because I never like to change things and take panic measures until I am sure there is a problem. Now I had to evaluate where my game was and what I had to do. Those five Test matches taught me that, yes, I could score runs in Australia and that I wasn't far away from being a good player.

And I had faced some of the all-time greats. I wasn't up against Shane Warne much because, other than in Perth, I didn't score that many runs, but when I did face him I really enjoyed the experience. Warne is a very good thinker about the game and tries to out-psych you. He tried to use his reputation against me and has such an aura about him. But he got me out just once and I don't think he got on top of me. He just never bowled any bad balls. He had that in common with Glenn McGrath, Brett Lee and Stuart Clark. They were all relentless.

The Australian batting wasn't bad, either. Ricky Ponting was undoubtedly the best batsman in the world at that time. I'd never seen anyone strike a ball so cleanly. He seemed to hit absolutely everything in the middle of the bat. I couldn't work out how he did it.

That Australia team could give any side from any era a run for their money. There wasn't a shadow of a doubt in my mind about that. But just because we were playing one of the best sides the world has seen didn't make it acceptable to lose 5–0. It never does.

I was not in the one-day squad that were to play against Australia and New Zealand afterwards, and I knew I wouldn't make the World Cup squad, so I thought, 'Right, I've got two months here. I'll have a couple of weeks off and then sit down to see where I can improve.' Off-stump was an area where they attacked me, so that was the best place to start.

For those two months, I spent hour after hour in the nets with a bowling machine and coaches Paul Grayson and Andy Flower for company, working on the area where it was now being said I might have a weakness. It wasn't so much a technical problem, I felt, but I looked at how Matthew Hayden and Justin Langer played balls outside their off-stumps and decided that I needed to replicate them.

Basically, when I played a cover drive I had a very straight bat and was technically correct, but in effect you are using just half of the bat when you play like that. I decided I needed to do it more the Australian way, which is to turn the bat slightly and play through the ball at an angle. I adjusted my batting position and hit ball after ball until it felt right. I nicked a few but kept practising and practising until it felt as though I had cured the problem.

I didn't want to make too big a deal of it. I just wanted to work it out for myself. The ball does naturally go across left-handers, so the circumstance was hardly anything new, but I had to sort it out and I was pleased to do so virtually in private at Chelmsford. As an England player, you are always in the spotlight and that includes when you practise. To be able to do something away from the media glare was beneficial to me.

I would have loved to be with the boys in Australia, finally enjoying a victory. Against all the odds, they won the one-day series, but that two-month period of practice and rest probably did me good. I was ready for the 2007 season, when we all hoped we could put the nightmare of the Ashes behind us and start afresh. It was a new beginning.

10

THE ART OF CAPTAINCY

In an early season challenge that I both relished and viewed as an intriguing development, I was made captain of the MCC for the curtain-raiser against the county champions, Sussex. Now a lot has been said about me possibly leading my country one day. Well, what can someone at my stage of life and career say about that? Of course, it interests me, and I've had captaincy experience at age-group level, but it doesn't drive me. It is not something I think about too much.

What was really good ahead of that early season game was that I was asked if I would like to talk to Mike Brearley, possibly the best captain of them all. Brearley is known as the brains behind England's famous 1981 Ashes success, the man who not only got the best out of Ian Botham, but proved himself a cerebral as well as imaginative leader.

I guess the mere fact that England wanted me to talk to the great man suggested that they might see me as captaincy material somewhere down the line and I can only be encouraged by that, even though it's a label I don't want to endorse, because it's such a long way off. In the short-term, this was an opportunity I was happy to grasp with both hands.

Not too long ago, players used to talk about the game a lot more after a day's play, invariably over a pint of beer, and you would learn things and swap views in the most convivial of circumstances. The game has changed and there is not so much of that these days, which is a shame in many ways for my generation, but the modern world is so competitive, and lived at such a fast pace, that there is often no time in a crowded calendar for gatherings such as that.

This was different. This was an audience with one of the greatest brains the game has known, and I wanted to lap up every second. I must say again, though, that I have always believed captaincy is something you work out for yourself. You can take on as much advice as possible and talk to as many people as you can, but at the end of the day you have to do things your way.

I was fascinated to ask Mike whether, for instance, he liked to attack a player's strengths or their weaknesses. He said that it depended on the situation and on your gut instincts. What quickly became evident is what a great man-manager Brearley is.

There is no real right or wrong way to captain a cricket side and when I came out of our meeting that's the thought that was uppermost in my mind. I have played under four differing and impressive captains already for England – Michael Vaughan, Paul Collingwood, Andrew Strauss and Andrew Flintoff – and you can learn from all of them. Brearley's *The Art of Captaincy* has become a textbook on how to lead a cricket side, and is as much about how to handle people as getting the tactics right, and that is very much how I see it. My dad bought that book for me when I was 14 but I'll be honest and say that I haven't read it properly yet – I was far more interested in Damon Hill's Formula One book at the time – but meeting Brearley and talking cricket for three hours was probably far more beneficial.

In English cricket promising players go into the national system so early that they never really have a chance to gain captaincy experience, certainly not at county level, and I can see that's a problem. One-time leading the MCC was not going to give me heaps of experience, but it was going to help.

The first thing I noticed when I was asked to captain the side was that both Steve Harmison and Matthew Hoggard were included in the team, which was going to be interesting for me. These two highly experienced members of the England side wasted no opportunity to take the mickey by sending me texts saying that they were going to refuse to do anything I asked them to do!

I enjoyed the banter and I enjoyed leading MCC. In a match like that, everyone has a personal and individual incentive for doing well, because they are either England players or players on the fringes of the side, and I had the total support of everyone in my first game as captain of a senior side.

To be honest, the captaincy wasn't a big deal. The team pretty much ran itself and I wasn't trying to impress with any particularly innovative or unusual decisions. The biggest thing for me was that I batted for five hours in the first innings to score 142 in our total of 425, and Hoggard, Harmison and Graham Onions bowled very well as Sussex replied with 385. The match petered out into a draw but it was a great start to the season.

The early weeks of the year continued to go well in the build-up to a summer that was to include Test series against the West

Indies and India. I was in the runs for Essex, benefiting from the hours I had spent in the nets, working on defending the outside off-stump. Meanwhile we were coming to terms with the departure of a man who had become a big part of the England set-up. Duncan Fletcher, arguably the most significant figure in the advancement of the England side between 1999 and the pinnacle of winning the Ashes in 2005, had decided to stand down after the disappointment of the Caribbean World Cup.

It's not for me to comment on what happened at the World Cup, but it was such a shame that Duncan's highly successful reign should end on the sad note of Ashes and World Cup failure. It had been obvious for a while that Duncan was going to go and I guess it was the right time not just for him but also for the team. We were starting afresh with a new man at the helm, and it was no surprise to any of us that the new coach was Peter Moores.

To me, he was always the outstanding candidate to step into such big shoes. I had worked with Peter a lot at the academy and his track record, both with the second string and, before that, at Sussex, was unbelievably good. He is incredibly enthusiastic and leaves nothing to chance and it seemed a natural progression that he should be promoted. Not only was Peter Moores the right man for the job, but he was a product of our system, proof that it worked.

You could say that Duncan and Peter are like chalk and cheese. Fletcher is very quiet and reserved whereas Moores is far more open. Duncan had a unique ability to spot a technical flaw, particularly with a batsman, but Peter knows everything about individual players, including all his statistics. Moores lives and breathes cricket. His energy is unbelievable and he gets far more involved than Duncan did in running training sessions, throwing everything into them. I knew Peter would be good and I knew he would change the culture, because perhaps things had started to get just that little bit stale.

Duncan Fletcher had an outstanding record, of course, and even though I worked with him only towards the end of his tenure, I felt compelled to listen to anything he told me, because he was so astute, which is always the sign of a good coach. Specifically, he taught me about the forward press method of playing spin bowling, something of a Duncan speciality, and the need to get my hands a bit lower when I batted.

Change is always needed in any sport after a while, however good the coach is, because there has to be a limit to how much one person can pass on, and how often he can motivate a team. Sir Alex Ferguson is obviously an exception to this, and is still winning after more than 20 years with Manchester United, but in most cases there comes a time when you put a line under all that has been done and move on. This was the right time for that to happen to the England cricket team.

The other significant news was that Andy Flower was to become Peter's number two and specialist batting coach. There are two things to say about this. The first is that this was a real blow for Essex. Andy was an extraordinarily talented player, clearly still good enough to score runs in county cricket for some time to come. We had lost Darren Gough to Yorkshire, Ronnie Irani to injury and now Andy to England, all in a short space of time, and that loss of experience was going to leave a big hole in my county side.

However, from an England point of view it was terrific news. Andy is very like Peter in the way he thinks about the game and they dovetail very well. I couldn't resist smiling to myself because Andy knew my game extremely well and was a good friend. Knowing someone who was new to the set-up, and with whom I had a rapport, had to be good for me. Apart from anything else, when someone new comes in, you usually have to start all over again with a person you don't know. I knew Andy was an excellent coach and an excellent person and I was delighted with his appointment.

Ottis Gibson joined as bowling coach, and so the new coaching team had defined areas of responsibility. I like talking about batting to other players because you can always pick up on little things here and there, but if there is anything specific that I'm concerned about, I would go to Andy. The bowlers have built a very good relationship with Ottis while Peter Moores oversees the whole thing. Then, early in 2008, Richard Halsall arrived as English cricket's first specialist fielding coach. That coaching set-up is likely to take the England team forward for a number of years. I think any new regime takes time to become fully established, possibly as long as three or four years for results to be seen, but they will come.

Meanwhile, life at my county was changing, too. However much of my time is devoted to the national cause, I am very keen to retain my links with Essex. The departures of Flower, Irani and Gough ushered in a new era. When Mark Pettini was chosen to succeed Ronnie Irani and work alongside new coach Paul Grayson, he went from fringe player to Essex captain after just one full season of county cricket. Mark, also known as 'Swampy', is one of my best friends in the team, and we have shared a house in the Chelmsford area since the summer of 2005. Taking over as the youngest Essex captain of all time, at the age of 24, was an enormous challenge for him.

In many ways, 2007 turned out to be a very hard year for Mark, and I found it strange not being able to do anything to help him, knowing that I would have been there beside him if I had not been playing for England. To be honest, I didn't think he should have taken the job at such an early stage of his career but now, a year on, I can see that it was good both for him and Essex.

If you had asked Mark a few months before his appointment whether he would become captain of Essex, he would have laughed, but it all happened very quickly. It is very much an Essex thing to promote from within at times of change, and it was exciting for him, because he had the chance to mould a young team in his own image and encourage players of promise to step up. He was able to shoulder the responsibility of moving Essex forward.

I was keen to be involved as much as possible, even from the outside, and I tried to offer any advice I could to Mark without being too pushy. I just wanted to be there for him and do my little bit to help advance the cause. I think as time goes on, and with some good young players around, this will turn out to be the start of a very successful period for Essex.

And the start of the 2007 season was very successful for

England. We had to hit back after the winter and, without wishing to show them any disrespect, the West Indies were good opposition for us to face, because they were going through a transitional stage post Brian Lara.

After all the talk about my problems outside off-stump, and all the hard work I had put in to try to solve them, I couldn't have wished for a better start to the Test season than a hundred and a man of the match award in the first game of a four-match series at Lord's.

We were expected to win, and probably would have done so if weather had not played a part in turning the match into a draw, but the most notable aspect of what was a satisfactory performance from England was a first innings that contained no fewer than four individual centuries. We have been criticized for not getting enough first-innings hundreds but this time, as well as for me, there were centuries for Paul Collingwood, Ian Bell and, on debut, Matt Prior, who played absolutely brilliantly and with great fluency after being brought into the side as wicketkeeper-batsman.

West Indies may have been considered to be a shadow of the side who dominated the world game for such a long time, but their bowling, notably when Fidel Edwards came into the side, was pretty quick and hostile, and for us to get 553 for five declared was a terrific start for the new coaching team, a great way to put the winter behind us and a terrific fillip for me.

The big scoring theme continued as West Indies replied with 437, Monty Panesar taking six early season wickets, five of them lbws. Then Kevin Pietersen became our fifth centurion of the match, and I registered a second innings

65, as we attempted to score runs quickly and give ourselves enough time to bowl West Indies out to win the match.

The rain ensured that was not to be, but we made up for lost time in the Second Test at Headingley when we welcomed back Michael Vaughan, who had returned for the World Cup but then had to miss the First Test with a finger injury.

This was the first time I had played under England's most successful Test captain and I was looking forward to it. Michael Vaughan demands respect, not just because he is the captain who won the Ashes for England, but also because he has such authority and is clearly highly regarded by the England players.

I quickly realized that Michael has the ability to create the right atmosphere within a team. He was always calm and collected, and never afraid to tinker in the field or be innovative with his field placings. He can treat the twin impostors of triumph and disaster just the same, and for a team it is far better to have a captain who transmits cool-headedness rather than one who kicks and screams when things go wrong. The best thing I can say about Vaughan's brand of leadership, I guess, is that he makes you feel comfortable playing in his team, and I think that is what a good captain does, even though he is not afraid to tell someone if they are not doing what he wants them to do, or to make the hard decisions.

It may have been assumed that Michael was under pressure when he returned to take over the captaincy from Andrew Strauss, but the players certainly didn't see it that way. Vaughan was the captain, deserved to be, and everyone was delighted to see him back.

You could tell what it meant to the team when the captain made a century in that comeback match on his home ground. Vaughan had been out of Test cricket for something like 18 months with a knee injury that could have ended his career. He watched on the sidelines while the England team, his England team, had played, and quite often struggled without him. Throughout all the solitary fitness work and bad times, when he might have questioned whether he would ever get back to the very top again, Michael Vaughan would have dreamed about returning to Test cricket with a century.

When he did so, Kevin Pietersen jumped on him and the England dressing room went mad. It was a lovely moment, not only for the captain but also for the team. We needed something to warm us up because that match in Leeds turned out to be one of the coldest on record for Test cricket. It was absolutely freezing and you could only pity the West Indies boys because this certainly wasn't Caribbean weather! The best way we found to try to combat the arctic conditions was to take hand-warmers out on to the field with us. They are used mainly in pre-season and are basically like warm tea bags that we put in our pockets, but it did lead to the slightly curious sight of the England team with their hands in their pockets at every opportunity!

Just as significant as the return of the captain was the return, in this case after six years, of Ryan Sidebottom. Matthew Hoggard's injury allowed one of the most consistent bowlers on the county circuit his chance, six years after he had played his solitary Test, and most people thought him to be a horses for courses selection to take advantage of any

THE ART OF CAPTAINCY

swing and seam that his old home ground had to offer. How wrong that assessment was.

Sidebottom turned out to be not a horse for a particular course, but a man for all seasons, a bowler who did so well on his return to international cricket that he went on to become England's player of the year – an amazing turnaround for a genuinely nice guy.

As Ryan began to establish himself, so the discussions about why he hadn't played for so long gathered apace. Duncan Fletcher must have had his reasons for not picking him – and it was widely assumed that Duncan felt Sidebottom wasn't quite quick enough – but word had got around on the circuit about Ryan's effectiveness and I think his early inclusion by Peter Moores was an indication that the new coach was going to pick people who were excelling in county cricket.

If Michael Vaughan scored a hundred and Ryan Sidebottom took eight wickets in the match as we recorded a thumping innings victory, they were both overshadowed by the biggest Test innings yet from Kevin Pietersen. Kevin's 226 proved, if any proof were needed, that he has the ability to destroy any bowling attack. He plays shots that I can only dream of playing. I've said it before, but he really does have the ability to become one of England's greatest ever batsmen.

It was an important victory. We needed to get back to winning ways and we continued in the same vein at both Old Trafford in the Third Test and Durham in the Fourth to take the series 3–0, the perfect start to the summer for us.

Manchester's storm in a teacup, which frankly meant little to the players, was a pre-match story involving Michael

Vaughan, Andrew Flintoff and use of the word 'Fredalo' in relation to England's poor World Cup performance. Monty Panesar and Steve Harmison again bowled well on a hard and quick wicket, just as they had done against Pakistan at Old Trafford a year earlier.

There was another century for me, this time in the second innings, and an excellent rearguard from the West Indies in the final innings. They fell just 60 runs short of their target of 454 thanks in the main to the extraordinary Shivnarine Chanderpaul, who was close to impossible to dismiss throughout the series.

The West Indies had four wickets in hand on the last day, and there were those who wondered whether history was about to be made, but when the opposition are chasing that many, you are always confident that you will be all right in the end, as indeed we were, even though Chanderpaul finished unbeaten on 116. When you have to grind your way to victory like that, it is often even more rewarding than making all the running in the match, and our feelings of satisfaction afterwards were added to by the fact that the series was ours. Any Test series win is a significant achievement for any cricketer.

Durham was similarly satisfying, even though the earlier cold of Leeds had by now given way to wet weather, which made the North-East Test a thoroughly soggy experience – not that Paul Collingwood minded because he scored a hundred on his home ground, and England won by seven wickets.

A good job well done is how I would describe the series. Okay, perhaps West Indies were not the strongest but they showed enough promise to give hope to those who want cricket in the Caribbean to be restored to its former health. The only critical comment I would make about myself is that, even though I was delighted to score two centuries in the series, I had still to kick on to a really big hundred.

I guess that's the next step in my career, but I don't think it's a question of a mental problem for me, failing to convert my hundreds into big ones or doubles. After all, I have got some big scores for Essex, so I think it's just one of those things at the moment. Graham Gooch always told me that the first 50 is the hardest, the second 50 is the second hardest, the third one is slightly easier and the fourth is yours to cash in. I hope the day when I cash in will come soon.

Although my game is more suited to Test cricket, I want to play in one-day matches, and I really think I can play both forms of the game. Hence I was delighted with a century I scored for Essex against Surrey at Whitgift School. I think it proved the key to me being selected for the one-day series against the West Indies, so the timing could not have been better. I batted through the innings for my first limited-overs hundred and was subsequently called up by England for the two Twenty20 matches and three limited-overs internationals that followed the Test series. It was good for me to play in the Twenty20 matches, even though the game doesn't exactly suit my style.

The rise and rise of Twenty20 cricket has gained momentum over the last year and it is clearly a game that the players and spectators enjoy. The way the game is going, you will definitely see more kids batting aggressively with all the money in Twenty20. But I sincerely hope and believe that Test cricket will remain the most significant form of the game. Yes, a good limited-overs game will always be great fun, and Twenty20 has increased that feel-good factor, but it is Test matches that people remember, and I hope it will always be that way.

That series marked the start of the split-captaincy system, with Paul Collingwood taking over from Michael Vaughan for the shorter forms of the game, a transition that seemed to be made very smoothly. The thing about those two is that they are friends and there is no ulterior motive to anything they do. Michael was quite happy to give up the one-day captaincy while Colly will never do anything to undermine the Test captain. It is a relationship that, as I write, is working well.

We shared the mini Twenty20 series and then lost the 50-over series, despite winning the first match at Lord's, which was quite a disappointment, but this was a young side under a new captain and there were enough encouraging signs to believe that we were moving in the right direction. I didn't score many runs, and I think that perhaps my shot selection wasn't the greatest at times, but I was still an inexperienced one-day player. I need to play as much one-day cricket as possible to establish myself in that form of the game.

So the early season was, in the main, good, but the second half of 2007 was much more eventful. The series against India had everything.

11

THE JELLY-BEAN AFFAIR

England's Test series against India in 2007 was a closely fought affair, full of drama, controversy and great cricket. It had everything except, unfortunately, an England victory. Even though we triumphed in a fantastic one-day series against India, the Test campaign is one we look back on with more than a little regret, because we really should have earned a share of it, but instead England lost their first home Test series since Australia toured in 2001. We allowed that proud record of success, mainly achieved under Michael Vaughan, to slip through our fingers.

It was, almost certainly, the last series in England for some greats of the world game, including Sachin Tendulkar, Sourav Ganguly, Anil Kumble and Rahul Dravid. It was also the series that, bizarrely, became dominated by a handful of jelly beans.

As the First Test at Lord's approached, there was considerable uncertainty over our bowling attack. Steve Harmison was suffering with a hernia problem and Matthew Hoggard had a back spasm in the build-up to the first day. That meant that we went into the game against one of the most formidable batting line-ups in world cricket with our most inexperienced attack in years. Jimmy Anderson came in for his first home Test in almost three years and Chris Tremlett, who wasn't in the original squad, made his Test debut ahead of Stuart Broad. It was also the first time that England had gone into a Test without any of the five bowlers who had won them the Ashes in 2005.

I think there was a general air of pessimism outside of our camp about our chances of bowling India out, but we had no doubts that we still had the ammunition for the job, and the inexperienced lads did outstandingly well after we had been bowled out for 298. I was annoyed to get out to one of Ganguly's little swingers for 36. That lbw decision gave rise to speculation that I may have over-compensated for my earlier problems outside off-stump. Andrew Strauss batted really well for his 96 and was unlucky not to go on to his first century in 42 innings.

Then it was the turn of the young lads. Jimmy, one of my best friends in the England side, showed what he could do and I was delighted for him as he took five wickets. Ryan Sidebottom's success story continued with four more, and Tremlett's bounce proved problematical for India as he claimed Wasim Jaffer's wicket, his first in Test cricket.

India had been bowled out for 201 and it was game on, even though the weather was not helping. I was lbw again in the second innings, this time to the more conventional swing of Zaheer Khan, who was to go on to have an outstanding series and prove a key figure in the summer, but Kevin Pietersen hit a century and we were in a good position to put pressure on India on the last day.

The weather forecast for that Monday was dreadful but it stayed dry for much of the day as we worked our way, slowly but surely, through the Indian batting line-up. There was some talk afterwards about our over rates but, quite honestly, considerable thought went in to taking wickets and there was no point in rushing through the overs just because the weather forecast was bad. As we all know, the forecasters can get it wrong and, in the end, it was not until tea that bad light became an issue.

A perilously close lbw shout by Monty Panesar to dismiss last man Sri Sreesanth was turned down by umpire Steve Bucknor, and if Monty had taken that last wicket, as we all believed he should have done, nobody would have been talking about England's over rates. It just would not have become an issue. I certainly don't think that was the reason why we drew the game. Soon after, the rain, which had affected the Test throughout, came down to save India from what we felt would be a thoroughly deserved defeat. Too much time had been lost, despite the fantastic new drainage system at Lord's, and we went to Trent Bridge for the Second Test, convinced that we would be able to push home our advantage.

However, as it turned out, this was one of India's best away wins in their history of 200 Tests abroad. It featured outstanding swing bowling from Zaheer Khan and R.P. Singh, and a century of the highest quality by Michael Vaughan, but there was so much more to it than that, including controversy, some bad feeling between the sides and, above all, 'jelly-beangate', surely one of the strangest scandals ever to hit a cricket match.

Where to begin? Well, more rain delayed the start of the game and India won a very important toss. I was very disappointed to get out lbw to Ganguly again, but perhaps I was getting a little too far across off-stump. I was our top scorer with 43 as we were bowled out for 198 in what, to be fair to us, were perfect bowling conditions. By the time we came to bowl, the conditions were much more conducive to batting, and India made full use of them.

With the benefit of hindsight, I guess it was an honour for a young player to be on the same pitch as the great Sachin Tendulkar when he was scoring runs, because there might not be too many more opportunities to experience that. He wasn't at his majestic best, because our bowlers did a very good job on him throughout the summer, yet Tendulkar scored 91 before he was out lbw to Paul Collingwood. By that time, he had done his job, India, with solid contributions all the way down their order, had reached 481 and we were well behind.

It was on the third evening, when Zaheer walked out to bat, that the game started to have a bit of edge in it. Test cricket is a highly competitive game, and that is how it should be. I guess there was a feeling within the Indian camp that they may have allowed themselves to be bullied a bit on some previous tours and they had no intention of letting that happen again. But what sparked off the incident that became the talk of cricket was just a prank. Okay, it was a childish prank, and we apologized for it afterwards, but we really didn't think it would cause such offence. Jelly beans are sweets that we have eaten on the field for some time. They are a good source of energy when we need a sugar intake and I would say most of the players eat them during games at various stages.

Earlier that summer, someone had thrown two or three jelly beans down on to the wicket when Shivnarine Chanderpaul of the West Indies had been batting, not for any reason other than a silly joke, and he just smiled, swept them off the wicket with his bat and carried on with the game. I think it was because he knocks a bail into the ground to take guard and someone decided to put sweets there for when he did that – silly stuff but pretty harmless. It's the sort of that can happen in county cricket but which is more unusual in the Test game, basically because the stakes are so high.

When Zaheer was batting at Trent Bridge, three jelly beans were kicked on to the wicket in his crease, more by luck than anything, and Zaheer smiled and knocked two of them away. Soon after that, he edged a ball through the slips for four and things started getting a little more heated, and verbal, between the players. Then Zaheer noticed the third jelly bean, which was still lying there on the wicket, and he must have assumed that we had put it there after his shot. Well, he took great offence and it all kicked off from there.

Firstly, he pointed his bat at Kevin Pietersen, which was a bit out of order, and Kev told him he had got the wrong guy. Then it got very heated and, in the aftermath, plenty was written in the press, fingers were pointed at potential culprits and the whole incident was blown out of all proportion.

The prime suspect, it appeared, was me. Yes, apparently I was the man who threw jelly beans on the pitch and enraged Zaheer to such an extent that, for a while, it got a bit out of hand. Why was I suddenly implicated? I was fielding at short leg so was seen in the vicinity of the 'crime' without a strong alibi. I think it was one of the radio or TV commentators who first claimed that it was me, perhaps because of something they had picked up on the stump microphone, a device that was to become a major talking point during this Test.

Well, I can exclusively reveal that it wasn't me. Honest. The case of mistaken identity didn't bother me too much. I think the England camp were just amused at how 'serious' the whole thing had become, even though the apologies offered to Zaheer were entirely genuine because he had clearly been upset by it all.

I had to laugh when my head, along with those of Jimmy Anderson and Matt Prior, appeared as jelly beans on the back page of one of the tabloids after the game. Michael Vaughan rang me to ask if I'd seen the paper and we had a smile about it, but it all became an unfortunate saga, not least for Matt Prior. He seemed to get more criticism than most for his behaviour in that match, again mainly because of the stump microphone.

This is a problem that needs to be addressed, because it really was irritating. An article appeared in one of the papers accusing Prior of uttering the following comment to one of the Indian players: 'I drive a Porsche. What do you drive?' A crass, unfunny remark you might say, and you would be right. Matt Prior never uttered it or anything like it, and this really does need to be corrected because it was very unfair to Matt.

Lots of things are said on the field, many of the comments being attempts at humour to keep everyone going at difficult times. One day, Matt had mentioned npower, the Test sponsors, and it had been picked up on television. So happy were the sponsors with this unexpected plug that they sent Matt a bottle of champagne, so we all thought we would have a bit of fun and mention as many sponsors as we could to see if they would send us any more freebies – more in jest, of course, than in expectation of actually receiving anything. At short leg, I muttered something about Bang and Olufsen televisions while Matt mentioned a Porsche. It was taken completely out of context, turned into some insult towards the Indians. That was unfair and wrong and it did make me wonder about the intrusiveness of the stump mics. I understand that they provide something of the atmosphere of the match for TV viewers, and it would be harsh to get rid of them. It's just that they need to be handled responsibly and turned down at the right times. As far as I'm aware, Matt is still driving his Skoda, so it didn't attract the attention of Mr Porsche anyway!

There were actually far more serious incidents in this match, including Sri Sreesanth bowling a beamer at Kevin Pietersen and then a no-ball bouncer at Paul Collingwood, delivered from round the wicket and from fully two yards in front of the crease. I suppose we have to give the young lad the benefit of the doubt on both of those, but the fact is that he was fined for a shoulder barge on Michael Vaughan in the same game.

What should be remembered, though, is how well our captain batted in the second innings. I wasn't around when Michael Vaughan batted as well as anyone in the world during that amazing series in Australia in 2002, but this innings in difficult circumstances offered a glimpse of how good a player he is. It was truly awesome and at one stage it looked as though it was going to put us right back in the match, at least until the captain was bowled in freak circumstances. That was pretty much that for us, even though Tremlett made the Indians work very hard for the 73 they needed to win in the fourth innings with some superb bowling that earned him three wickets.

So it ended in defeat for us, and lots of questions about whether we went too far in our competitiveness throughout the match. To me, the competitive edge made it a fantastic series to watch and play in. All the players on the pitch were proud to play for their country and that is going to lead to passionate, hard-fought cricket. At Trent Bridge, it also led to cricket of a very high standard. We may have crossed the line of unacceptable behaviour but I still think the series should have been remembered for the standard of cricket. There is nothing wrong with a bit of an edge in the game, not least because I think supporters love to see tough cricket, and so do I.

We had to go to The Oval to try to salvage the series, a venue where our chances were not helped by it being the usual belter of a pitch, one on which it was always going to be hard to force a result. Our hopes of doing just that took another blow when we lost the toss and were sentenced to hard toil in the field. India's powerful batting line-up proved their mettle and were devilishly hard to get out. Of all the great talents in their side, however, the identity of their only century maker in a total of 664 was quite hard to predict. Anil Kumble has been an awesome leg-spin bowler but has not been renowned for his ability with the bat. Here, though, he scored his maiden Test century, and to all intents and purposes our series was over.

It was vitally important, however, for us to continue to

fight like mad in this game, to show that there wasn't much between the sides as much as anything else. For me, this match was disappointing because I got two starts and didn't convert them into hundreds. No excuses. Once I had got to 61 and 43 I should have gone on to a century. At least I wasn't out lbw in this game, but that didn't offer much consolation.

We batted reasonably well as a team, though, and drew the match with ease, which meant something to us. It was very hard not to look back at Lord's and say that we should have won that match and, if we had done so, we would have drawn the series. There are always so many ifs and buts, and that sums up sport, but we didn't think that India were any better than us. A proud unbeaten record had been lost and we needed to hit back as strongly as we could in the following one-day series.

I was anxious about my one-day place because I hadn't exactly set the world alight against the West Indies on my return to the limited-overs side, so my century in the first match against India at the Rose Bowl was very gratifying. It made me feel that I deserved to be there, and it was so reassuring because it proved to me that I could perform at one-day level.

The Rose Bowl has never been a particularly happy hunting ground for me but this was a top day, with Ian Bell joining me in scoring his maiden one-day hundred and Andrew Flintoff, back in the side, bowling at 90 miles per hour. Bell is one of the most naturally gifted players in the game. Some of the drives he played were of the highest class and made the art of batting look so easy. For me, the century was a significant landmark but I was actually more pleased with my one-handed catch in the gully because it showed that I was improving in the field.

We won and won well at Hampshire and so started a very pleasing one-day series for us, which we went on to win 4–3, Paul Collingwood's first series win as one-day captain. India won a high-scoring match at Bristol, we won comfortably at Edgbaston and then Ravi Bopara and Stuart Broad saw us to victory at Old Trafford when it looked as though we were going to be on the receiving end of another defeat. The series was going our way but India hit back with victories at Headingley and in an extraordinary match at The Oval before we won the decider at Lord's, a match for which, unfortunately, I was left out.

So it was an eventful summer, a good one for me and, on the whole, for England, generating a lot of experiences and information to analyse and store in the bank.

12
WINNING AWAY

Missing the first-ever World Twenty20 Cup in South Africa at the start of the 2007–08 winter was a disappointment, but I could hardly complain, because I had such little experience of that form of cricket. There was a bit of a clamour in the media for Twenty20 specialists, the guys who had thrived in domestic Twenty20 matches and gained considerable experience in this new game.

I could understand the argument, and in a way it was good that players such as Darren Maddy, Chris Schofield, Vikram Solanki, Jeremy Snape and James Kirtley were selected as it gave them a great chance to play in a great tournament at the highest level. In my experience, there's nothing like international cricket.

The tournament did not go well for England but there was plenty to look forward to. The first half of the winter was to be made up of two separate tours to Sri Lanka, the first a one-day trip followed by a month at home and then a return for a three-Test series.

This was the first time that a tour to the same country had been split up this way and it was a welcome development, if only because it made the demands of touring that little bit easier. I would never complain about life as an England player because we are so privileged, but there is no question that itineraries are becoming ever busier and this seemed to me like a sensible move forward.

It also meant that, when we left for three one-day matches in Dambulla and two in Colombo, we could devote our thinking totally to limited-overs cricket – a one-day squad playing solely one-day cricket helped create a single-minded attitude. The concise 15-day trip was conducive to intense, hard work.

We had beaten India in one-day cricket but this was likely to be very different. Sri Lanka away is one of the toughest propositions in cricket. This was to be the one-day game played, in some cases in extreme heat, on slow, low pitches that were not likely to give any assistance to the bowlers.

With a good warm-up match under our belts, we travelled to Dambulla, which is in the heart of the Sri Lankan jungle and a very picturesque, quiet spot. The lovely hotel we stayed at was used mainly by honeymooners and I'm afraid their tranquillity was interrupted by a bunch of loud sportsmen taking over the place for a week, but I hope we didn't spoil their fun, or that of the monkeys that strode around the place trying to get into everyone's rooms!

The drive from Colombo to Dambulla was a bit hairy. How there are not more accidents in Sri Lanka goodness knows. When we finally arrived, with the more nervous in our party still recovering from the five-hour roller-coaster ride, we were greeted by a deadpan David Lloyd, the former England coach and now Sky commentator, asking why we didn't take the motorway, which was much quicker and easier. There was, of course, no motorway but some members of our group fell for Bumble's wind-up, which was backed up by our team manager, Phil Neale, who explained, with a straight face, that the toll was quite expensive on the motorway and the ECB were not prepared to pay it. I think some of the more gullible types believed for the rest of our trip that the stingy ECB were stopping us taking the best route on our travels!

The Dambulla wicket looked slow but an absolute belter, and we went into the first one-day international expecting scores of 300 plus to be common-place in this five-match series. So we were delighted to restrict Sri Lanka to 269. And when Phil Mustard, making his England debut, and I got us off to a reasonable start, we felt we were very much in the hunt. But Farvez Maharoof came on to bowl his little cutters and take the pace off the ball, and suddenly it became much harder to score runs, and we all got bogged down, myself included. When we were dismissed for 150, it was not only a massive disappointment but it led to dire predictions of a 5–0 thrashing for us, just like the one we suffered at home in 2006.

We had lost six one-day matches on the trot to Sri Lanka and drastic action was needed. Clearly the wickets were not going to be anything like as good for run-making as we had envisaged, and we were going to be playing on the same Dambulla square for the next two matches. It was now that Ottis Gibson, our bowling coach, came into his own. He, along with Peter Moores, conducted some full and productive meetings with the bowlers on how we could replicate what their bowlers were doing. It was to lead to a quite spectacular turnaround.

Beforehand, we had all believed that traditional back of a length one-day bowling was going to be the order of the day, but now we realized that taking the pace off the ball, cutting it and then slipping in the odd variation of pace would serve the purpose better. There were only three days before the second game but the bowlers adapted outstandingly well. It was strange, really, to be involved in low-scoring, almost attritional 50-over matches so soon after the Twenty20 World Cup, but it was necessary to adapt to different conditions. When you turn up at Lord's or Old Trafford, you pretty much know what you are going to get. Playing overseas is that much harder because you are not entirely sure what awaits you. By the time of the second match, the adjustments had been made, we batted first and scored 234 – Owais Shah was to the fore with 82 – and then restricted Sri Lanka to 169 due to a great collective effort from the bowlers.

Back in the series against all expectations, we enjoyed a team night at the hotel watching the England rugby team beat Australia in the rugby World Cup. I love rugby as do Graeme Swann, who had a very good comeback series in Sri Lanka, and Kevin Pietersen, while Ryan Sidebottom is a big rugby league man.

It was fantastic watching the game in a big group environment on the big screen, not least because two members of our management party, security man Reg Dickason and media officer James Avery, are Australians by birth and honorary Englishman while they are involved with us! The pair are great characters and invaluable members of our back-up team but on this occasion they slipped off towards the end of the match to suffer alone because they knew what was coming in terms of the stick they would receive from us at the final whistle!

By the time of the third international you could see that Paul Collingwood was growing into the captaincy and learning all the time as a leader. He is very big on everyone knowing their role in the side and what is expected of them, which is vital in one-day cricket, and he speaks as someone who knows exactly what is expected of him as a player. Particularly in one-day cricket, Colly bats with the freedom of someone who is comfortable with his game and knows how to get the best out of himself. He is not a screamer and a shouter as a captain but leads by example, and he is hugely respected in our dressing room.

Meanwhile, I was getting used to working with my new opening partner Phil Mustard, the Colonel to one and all, after the Cluedo character. Much had been said about us not always taking advantage of the fielding restrictions in the power-play overs, but take a look at the statistics of our performances in Duncan Fletcher's regime and I think you'll find that we were only two or three runs behind the other leading sides over the course of a considerable amount of time.

The Colonel and I made a few starts in Sri Lanka without ever going on to the big one that we sought, but the wickets were hardly conducive to the sort of attacking strokeplay in which Mustard in particular specialized. Basically, Adam Gilchrist has raised expectations about keeper-batsmen, and top-order batters in general, but then he is one of the greatest talents to have played the game.

Phil is a proper north-easterner, a very amusing character

who impressed me with his keeping in Sri Lanka. He had an unorthodox style but he seemed to catch everything. Our batting as a partnership, and England's as a team, was okay, no more than that, but we won the third international in Dambulla to take a 2–1 lead in the series, and we did it chasing, which was much the harder way to win on these slow pitches under flood-lights. We restricted Sri Lanka to 164 and overhauled that total with just two wickets in hand. So we moved on to Colombo in a position that barely seemed credible after the first game.

And it was at the Premadasa Stadium that I enjoyed my best moment of the one-day trip when I scored 80, most of them in partnership with Kevin Pietersen, as we overhauled Sri Lanka's 211 to win the match and the series, a significant overseas victory. I was disappointed it wasn't a hundred but in a low-scoring series, 80 was good enough. I think our sense of achievement was even greater because of the circum-stances, and it wasn't spoiled by defeat in the dead rubber match with which this leg of the tour finished. Victory over France in the World Cup rugby semi-final, which we watched this time with a few beers because the series was won, was followed by a month off before we were due to return to Sri Lanka and a short holiday in Paris.

Defeat in the one-day series at home hit Sri Lanka hard and it would have been lovely to have done the double over them. We knew the Test series would be even harder, with a history of competitive, fiery cricket between England and Sri Lanka, and the biggest obstacle in front of us would be Muttiah Muralitharan, who was fit again after missing the one-dayers.

The scary thing for me ahead of the series was that I

couldn't actually pick Murali's variations. It was okay when I first faced him in 2006 but now, looking at DVDs of him and bearing in mind he had added the doosra to his armoury, I was finding it much more difficult. Perhaps it was the TV screen that was deceiving me but this was worrying. Murali seemed to be crouching after the moment of delivery and I couldn't get a proper sight of his wrist. I couldn't let it distract me, though, and the warm-up games went well ahead of the First Test in Kandy. We were ready to go.

As it turned out, I didn't have to worry about Murali at all in the First Test, and for the worst possible reason. I was out for a duck and four in that game, falling both times to Chaminda Vaas. After spending two weeks preparing to bat for a long time, this was not what I was hoping for or expecting. Maybe I was guilty of thinking too much about Murali and almost forgetting that Vaas is an extremely skilful, experienced bowler with plenty of Test wickets to his name. Maybe I just received two good balls at early stages of my innings. Whatever the reason, the First Test was not just disappointing for me but also for the whole England side as we lost a close and hard-fought match after coming extremely close to emerging with an honourable draw.

We were, in fact, just 20 minutes away from securing that draw when our final wicket fell. And it could have been even better than a draw after we dismissed Sri Lanka for 188 in their first innings, with Matthew Hoggard taking four wickets. At one stage, we had them on 42 for five. Despite my failure, we responded with 281. Ian Bell batted extremely well, but the unquestionable story of the innings, and the match, was

Murali overtaking Shane Warne's world record 708 wickets. It took me back to the tsunami game at The Oval a couple of years earlier, when I sat and watched Murali and Warne bowling at a single stump on the outfield, trying to outdo each other. It was amazing to watch.

We all knew it was coming and our aim was to stop him reaching this incredible landmark on his home ground in Kandy, but as the fireworks were set off around the Asgiriya Stadium after he had bowled Paul Collingwood to claim the record, none of us could begrudge this amazing bowler and genuinely nice man his truly historical moment. People talk about his action being dodgy and he is certainly a bit of a freak with his double-jointed wrists and elbows, but it actually doesn't look so bad from 22 yards as it does on TV. In any case, he has been cleared of doing anything illegal and his record is astonishing. There are not many geniuses around but Murali is definitely a bowling genius – and he is a genius who goes about his work with a smile on his face, even though that is probably because he knows he is going to get you out! On the rare occasions when he doesn't get a five-for, he gets a bit grumpy. He is close friends with Andrew Flintoff and some other members of the England team, and there was a lot of warmth towards him after this accomplishment.

Obviously, one of us was going to be the record-breaking victim and we had joked about who was due a benefit season because if it was him, he could get something signed and auction it! Colly was actually coming to the end of his benefit year, so maybe he could take a consolation out of it after all.

What really killed us was a great innings from that other

successful son of Kandy, Kumar Sangakkara, in the second innings. He had been a leading wicketkeeper-batsman for some years but by this time he had given up the gloves in Test cricket and it led to spectacular results for him with the bat. On this occasion, Sanga's 152 in a Sri Lankan second innings of 442 for eight was the decisive factor and meant that we had just over a day to chase 350, or survive.

A victory was a distinct possibility as far as we were concerned, especially when Bell and Matt Prior were going well, but in the end the draw was the more realistic target, so it was a huge blow when we couldn't quite hang on. The new ball coming an hour and a half before the close proved our eventual undoing. History told us that Nasser Hussain's England team came back from one down to win a three-Test tour of Sri Lanka, but we knew it was going to be very difficult to emulate that.

Not only did the match end in defeat for England, but it was one of my worst ever Tests, so the question arose, 'What do I do now?' The first thing was to have a good chat with Andy Flower about how I should respond to nicking off twice at such an early stage of a match. We decided to analyze the angle of Vaas's delivery and the fact that my head was moving a little too much to the off side and thus accentuating the threat that Vaas posed to me. I think that Vaas being a little bit slower than most other opening bowlers didn't help me. It was almost a case of having a little bit too much time to think about it. Vaas is a left-arm bowler with a fantastic record, and I think that Marcus Trescothick, another left-hander, also had a bit of trouble against him.

I spent four days with Andy in the build-up to the Second

Test in Colombo, working on the bowling machine and replicating Vaas's angle of delivery for ball after ball, hour after hour. I was concentrating on delaying my movement and letting the ball come to me, and all the while I was thinking, 'I need to score runs in the next match.'

It's amazing how cricket can play with your mind. I had felt so good in the build-up to the First Test but now, after one poor match, I suddenly felt very uncomfortable and lacking in confidence. Colombo looked the flattest of wickets, so I decided I had to grind it out as much as I could. I was determined not to give away my wicket, or make any mistakes.

In truth, the wicket at the Sinhalese Sports Club, the home of Sri Lankan cricket, was too good to get a result out of, even in five days. This game was a throwback, an old-fashioned match in which both sets of bowlers toiled away with precious little to show for their efforts. Stuart Broad made his debut, and if he goes on to play 150 Tests I doubt whether he will have tougher conditions in which to bowl.

We batted first and Michael Vaughan went off like a dream, as good as he had been against India at Trent Bridge the previous summer. When the captain had reached 80 I was on something like 20, so keen was I not to get out, but in the end we both fell in the eighties. Matt Prior again batted well for 79, but we were a little under par in reaching 351 all out. And I was disappointed with my lbw decision, although I know these things even themselves out.

I still couldn't pick Murali out of his hand, though, but I played him okay in the Second Test. The ball doesn't lie, as Marcus Trescothick once told me, so I tried to pick the line after it had left his hand, to see which way it was turning in the air. It was different facing Murali in his own backyard but I don't think he really enjoys bowling to left-handers, as his record proves, so that was in my favour. I had decided to sweep him but didn't really need to because I found I could tuck his doosra off my legs without too much difficulty.

If we fell a little short of where we might have been, you couldn't level that accusation against Sri Lanka. They replied with 548 for nine declared and their captain, Mahela Jayawardene, extended his incredible record on his home ground with 195. After Sangakkara's innings at Kandy, we understood that we were dealing with two batsmen who were world-class performers, at least in their own backyard.

There wasn't too much more that our bowlers could do. Stuart showed that he belonged at this level with gutsy bowling while Steve Harmison returned to the side, after missing Kandy, and bowled really well. We were under a little bit of pressure to bat out time in the second innings but the wicket really was the winner and we prepared to move on to Galle for our last chance to level the series and, more importantly, to play the first Test in this beautiful coastal spot since the tsunami claimed so many lives in that area.

However, the weather was so terrible that there was a real chance the Third Test would be played in Colombo instead. That's what we were told before we'd even left Colombo. Apparently, the outfield at the picturesque ground was under water and the rebuilt stadium wasn't going to be ready in time.

We travelled south anyway to stay in the beautiful Lighthouse Hotel, one of the best we stay in on the circuit, and when we arrived it wasn't quite as bad as I feared. Everybody had been saying that the match would definitely be off and we would have to go back at the SSC ground but, thank goodness, it never came to that. For the local people, it was really important for that game to be staged at Galle, and I think there was a will to put it on however difficult that was going to be.

You could say it was not exactly like turning up at Lord's before a Test. The outfield was muddy when we first went there three days before the match, the pitch was the same colour as the outfield and most of the stands had building work going on in them. But everyone was so pleased to see us and so enthusiastic about Test cricket coming back to their city.

After visiting Galle with the England A team just two months after the disaster had struck, I found it very emotional to see how things had developed. Everyone says something like that puts sport into perspective and it's absolutely true. We undertook various charity visits and projects before the match with an enthusiasm that you don't always see when sportsmen are confronted with extra-curricular duties.

At first, the ground didn't look much different from the way it had on my first visit, but the indoor school and pavilion were looking good and the rest of the ground gradually caught up in the days, and nights, leading up to the game. As we moved around the area and saw how much had been rebuilt and how the local community were somehow getting over the disaster, one constant thought was on our minds. Will we play? Can we play? We need to play because we are one down.

And we did play the Third Test, even though the rain never

really went away throughout our trip, just before Christmas. We actually won what should have been a good toss and we were all convinced that what must have been a really unprepared pitch would be very difficult to bat on. Maybe we chased wickets too much or maybe it was just amazing how quickly the pitch dried out in the sun but it played a lot better than we thought it would – so much so that Sri Lanka reached 499 for eight declared with Jayawardene scoring a double century and we were up against it.

What we didn't expect, though, was to be bowled out for 81 in our first innings. This was a real low for us and led, for the first time in my experience, to some of our supporters getting restless and even a few of them booing as we got on our coach outside the ground at the end of the day's play. Yes, we'd had a really bad day but that can happen in sport. We had lost momentum in the field, we had lost Michael Vaughan early on and then I had run out Ian Bell.

He was gutted and I felt guilty, but of course I didn't mean to do it. It's like when you drop a catch. Nobody means to make a mistake, and ideally, in this instance, I would have been the one to go because it was my fault, but it was one of those 'yes, no, oh shit' moments when Bell was the victim of my calling and a direct hit.

It was a bad experience. Our support is usually fantastic but here we not only had people complaining to us in the ground but they were also coming up to us in the hotel that night, saying, basically, 'We've spent a lot of money and come all this way to watch this rubbish.' What can you do in those circumstances? No one could ever accuse an England side of not trying. All we could say in reply was that we were sorry and we would try to turn it around. You do feel sorry when people have spent so much, but we as a side are definitely more disappointed. It is one of the great things about cricket that there is still contact between England players and supporters in this day and age, because it's not always the case with other sports, but it can be something of a tour of duty. From the moment you wake up on an England tour to the moment you go to bed, people think it is their right to come up and chat to you and, without being rude, that can be a bit wearying. It can be nice to return to anonymity in my little Essex village. It can be an escape.

It should be said that our support is magnificent 99.9 per cent of the time. Even during the Ashes when we lost 5–0, our supporters were amazing and stuck with us the whole time. I'm sure that any disappointment among our fans in Galle was more than matched in the media, where I imagine everyone had their knives out for us. At times like that, it's good that we can't see the papers.

The next day at the ground, a big banner proclaimed 'thanks England for 15 wasted days', which wasn't the most reassuring thing to see, but we were encouraged that the Barmy Army had decided to offer a show of support and come up with a banner of their own, backing Michael Vaughan and the England team. That meant a lot to us.

I like to think we showed our resilience second time round in earning a draw from that match, with a little help from the weather. We have characters in our side who will not lay down and die. We may get beaten at times but it's never a case of, 'We'll give it away and we'll be all right tomorrow.' There is much more to this England side than that.

I'm pleased to say I scored a hundred in that rearguard action. It meant an awful lot to me not only to help my country but also to register three figures in such a significant match for the people of Sri Lanka. It was a bit of a grind but that was okay by me, and whatever happens in my career I can say I scored a hundred in the second innings of a Test against Murali in his own backyard – not only that but it was my seventh Test century three days before my 23rd birthday and I was informed that only Don Bradman and Sachin Tendulkar had scored more than that at the same age. Someone had told me before the series that if I scored two centuries in Sri Lanka, I would have actually drawn level with Bradman, ahead of Sachin, and I had even talked to Jimmy Anderson about it, but I think it would have been slightly unfair on the great man if I had sneaked into his company!

Reaching a landmark like that does make you wonder what lies in store in the future. I think I can safely say that I won't end up averaging 99 in Test cricket as Bradman did! But I hope to score a lot more runs and it will be nice to look back and remember achievements such as this one. It certainly felt like a nice thing to have under my belt, and made the turkey taste that much better back in England on Christmas Day, which is also my birthday. I had, at least, made one big score in Sri Lanka, done my little bit for the side, and that gave me some satisfaction rather than the bad feeling you get when you don't pull your weight for the team.

That was no consolation for losing the series, though. We

had now lost two Test series on the trot, which had never happened under Michael Vaughan's captaincy before. In mitigation, lbw decisions had not gone our way against India, when we felt we had earned a share of the series, and Sri Lanka is a notoriously hard place to play. I certainly think it was unfair of Mahela Jayawardene to criticize us at the end of this series.

Basically, the Sri Lankan captain said that we were too negative and had talked ourselves out of the series by saying that it was going to be tough. Well, what were we supposed to say? That we were going to win easily? That would have been totally arrogant. We were confident enough going into that series but that doesn't mean we were going to shout it from the rooftops.

It was a little disappointing, to be honest. I have respect for all opponents, win or lose, and to me you don't go shouting your mouth off at the end of a series when you know that you are not going to face that opposition again for a few years. Yes, he is a great player and decision-maker and he is quite fiery on the pitch, which is fine, but so are the Aussies and they are perfectly sporting and gracious to their opponents off it.

I was content with my work and the fact that we had succeeded in our damage limitation exercise. Every Test result is important and, even though the series was lost, it was satisfying to draw at Galle.

It was time to take stock as we headed home for Christmas. As it transpired, Matt Prior was to be dropped after this, which came as something of a surprise to me. Matt didn't need to be told that he had dropped a couple of catches, mainly off Ryan Sidebottom, but we were talking about three back-to-back Tests in the heat and humidity of Sri Lanka. It was natural that mistakes would be made towards the end of that run.

What we were seeing was an indication that the new regime were not afraid to be ruthless, as would be further demonstrated in the second half of our winter programme in New Zealand. Matt is a gutsy player and his batting in Sri Lanka was fantastic, so the last thing he needed was the press going on about how he made a couple of mistakes. I would not be surprised at all if he bounced back to have a very successful England career.

A lot of people suggested that it was the reaction of Sidebottom to errors in the field off his bowling contributed to Matt's demise but I disagree. What you need to know about 'Siddy' is that he is one of the nicest men in the world who just happens to show his emotion on the pitch. It's as if he just cannot help himself – nothing personal and only because he wants to succeed. Graeme Swann knows him well from Nottinghamshire and he says that Ryan has always been the same. You think he's having a go at you if you even misfield off his bowling, but then you realize you just have to let him be. It's because he cares so much. Siddy will apologize when we come off but you know he doesn't mean it. It's just that he turns from Siddy the nice guy to Siddy the growly bowler, and everybody loves him for who he is.

Ravi Bopara, whom I knew really well from our time at Essex and throughout age-group cricket, was given his Test debut in Sri Lanka but, after a promising start, it did not go well for him and he ended the tour with three consecutive ducks. Ravi had the total opposite start to me in Test cricket.

I was so lucky to start well, which took the pressure off me, whereas he had it tough, including a freak run-out, but that doesn't make him a lesser player.

Ravi would have had a tough Christmas but even though he missed going to New Zealand when it was clear that Sri Lanka had affected his confidence, we again saw how good he was when he scored a remarkable double century for Essex against Leicestershire in the 2008 Friends Provident Trophy. He will be back at the highest level. For now, New Zealand awaited and I was looking forward to my first visit to that beautiful country.

13

BACK FROM THE BRINK IN NEW ZEALAND

I had a preconceived idea about New Zealand. I thought it would be like England was 30 years ago, and I was right, to an extent, in a good way. It soon became apparent that it was a beautiful place but very quiet, at least in Christchurch where we arrived one Thursday in January 2008 at the start of a two month one-day and Test tour.

My first thought was, 'Where is everyone?' This was the biggest city in the south island of New Zealand and there was no one about. It got a little busier when the English turned up but I always had a sense of, 'If we weren't here, I'm not sure anybody else would be,' and that included at the Test match grounds, which were taken over by English supporters.

New Zealand was definitely one of my favourite places to tour. In India it's a case of hotel room, cricket and not much else, but New Zealand was a bit more like Australia with beaches and plenty of things to do. It was almost like being in England and that makes you content within your environment and more likely to do well.

The priority going into the first leg of the tour was to

build on the progress we had made in beating both India and Sri Lanka in one-day cricket. I looked at the statistics and I think it's fair to say that it was a long time since England had won three one-day series in a row.

We knew New Zealand were very competitive, particularly in their own backyard, but they had no superstars. Brendon McCullum, who was to emerge as a world-class hitter, hadn't really caught fire by that stage.

The two warm-up games we played against Canterbury could not have gone better for me. In the second one, I played probably my best one-day innings to date, which was a bit of a waste in a way. I scored 70 odd in the first game and 140 in the second. I wished I'd saved that score for an international but it had to be good because it meant I was in good form and was taking confidence from my last innings in Sri Lanka.

At least it meant I was going in the right direction and I think quite a few people were surprised that I could dominate the bowling like that. I knew I could do it but it was a different kettle of fish to dominate international bowling at one-day level. Getting the better of Canterbury was not quite the real thing, but you want to get any tour off to a good start and I couldn't have asked for a better way to start this one.

And I hit a six! My first as an England player and one, I'm pleased to say, that went straight down the ground and over the boundary in the conventional big-hitting manner. Okay, I had a howling gale behind me but a straight six for your country is something to be relished. The immediate reaction in the dressing room was huge amusement. I had hit sixes for Essex but I'm not sure that any of my England colleagues thought that I could do it.

I had thrown my hat into the ring for the two Twenty20 internationals that started the tour in Auckland and Christchurch, and was disappointed to be left out of the team for those games, although I could understand the thinking. At that stage, Twenty20 wasn't a form of the game to which I was particularly suited, and I certainly could not argue with England's selection because we won both matches to get the tour off to a great start.

It did not take the media long to speculate that we would win every game against New Zealand, assuming that we would be too strong for them. We never thought that way and it's my belief the attitude showed disrespect towards the Black Caps. People seemed to forget that New Zealand were rated the third best one-day side in the world – and an interesting fact that was being completely ignored was that only Australia had won both one-day and Test series in New Zealand in recent years, so they were not exactly going to be a pushover.

I was back for the five-match one-day international series, the first three of which were staged at rugby grounds. They were played on drop-in pitches with no proper square around them and, consequently, I found it very hard to get the ball off the longer grass that constituted a square. I would hit the ball into the outfield and it would just die whereas in England it pings off. In the first match at Wellington, at the 'cake tin' rugby ground, I felt I was middling the ball and it wasn't going anywhere.

That game was a big disappointment to us but not nearly

as bad as the second match in Hamilton, where we were thrashed by ten wickets thanks to some explosive hitting from McCullum and an interesting newcomer to international cricket, Jesse Ryder. It soon became clear that Ryder was a very natural hitter, one of the new breed of batsman of whom I think we will see more and more in these days of Twenty20 cricket.

Jesse seemed to have a God-given talent for hitting the ball, one that not too many people have, but his excellent debut one-day series ended in most unfortunate circumstances when he put his arm through a window during a night out to celebrate the Kiwis win. Ryder was a bit of a loose cannon but he coped well when we let him have a few verbals to test his temperament at Hamilton. It will be interesting to see how he goes in Test cricket, when he will have a lot more balls round his ears to deal with.

The Black Caps wicketkeeper and opening batsman, Brendon McCullum, meanwhile, was emerging as a significant player. His technique of walking down the wicket towards a bowler was quite new in the game and provided another challenge for us to consider. It takes some talent to walk down the wicket towards bowlers such as Jimmy Anderson and Stuart Broad and play them from 17 or 18 yards. The tendency would be to bowl short at him, and there was a feeling that McCullum might be susceptible to the shorter ball, but every time our guys delivered one of those, he proved to be a capable hooker. He was finding a method that worked extremely well for him. This wasn't slogging. This was extremely good batting and it took us some time

Cutting the great Shane Warne for four during the Ashes series of 2006–07, which was to turn into a horrible 5–0 defeat for us.

Andrew Flintoff, as stand-in captain, had to bear the brunt of the criticism after our Ashes whitewash.

Dirty looks were always a part of Shane Warne's armoury, and he is clearly not impressed with my batting here!

Right and below In one of the more bizarre controversies to engulf cricket, Zaheer Khan took great offence to jelly beans being thrown on to the pitch at Trent Bridge. Here he looks for the sweets along with his captain Anil Kumble and umpire Ian Howell. For a while, I was prime suspect in the great 'who threw them' mystery. Not guilty, your honour!

Arms held aloft, I celebrate my maiden one-day century with Ian Bell, against India at the Rose Bowl. It was another significant box ticked.

Double vision – some have said Andrew Strauss and I are too similar to open the batting together but we put on a hundred in our first Test back at the top of the order against New Zealand at Lord's.

right Test series wins produce the most satisfying feeling in cricket. Jimmy Anderson and I take part in the lap of honour at Trent Bridge after we defeated New Zealand 2–0.

below left I am now a Test bowler, having turned my arm over against South Africa at Lord's.

below right I have not spent enough time on my music over the years but the saxophone is one of the instruments I can play. Perhaps I'll take it up again.

Above The biggest controversy of the 200[season occurred wher Ryan Sidebottom collided with Grant Elliott, whom we then ran out. Paul Collingwood made a mistake but I defy anyone to say for sure he would not have do[the same.

Left Kevin Pietersen has extraordinary tale and his two switch-hit for six off Scott Styris Durham took the gam to another level.

ove left One of the
ost successful
ptains of recent
ars, Michael Vaughan
signed from the
ptaincy during the
ries against South
rica.

ove right Peter
oores left his position
the end of Kevin
etersen's captaincy.

ght Leaving the field
ter my long-awaited
ntury that ended a
riod of regularly
ing dismissed in the
ties and sixties.

Above New coach Andy Flower and new captain Andrew Strauss bonded well from the word go.

Left Meeting the Queen during the match at Lord's added to the sense of occasion.

ove My 96 at Lord's
as a great moment for
e, but I just wish I
uld have added those
tra four runs.

ght The eleven overs
intoff bowled on the
st day at Lord's were
nongst the finest I
ve ever seen.

Playing my part: I catch Hussey off Swann, sealing our victory over Australia. There's no feeling that can compare with winning the Ashes. I will be keeping the ball and making sure it takes pride of place at my house.

before we discovered we could contain him by bowling tighter at him.

That Hamilton one-dayer, which left us two down in the series with three to play, was a real low point in our tour, and it led to some harsh words during a full and frank discussion in the dressing room. We hadn't seen Peter Moores open up and express his feelings before, after nine months in the job. Peter had a reputation for being tough and taking no nonsense during his time as Sussex coach, but this was the first time that the England players saw that side of him. It was fully justified. You have to remember that coaches are under just as much pressure as players and they are dependent on us to produce the goods for them. When things don't go well, it's rather like football in that the buck stops with the coach, and Peter felt that this was the right time to deliver a wake-up call. He was absolutely correct.

New Zealand hit us like a bombshell in that game and plenty of soul-searching ensued as we discussed how we had let it happen. When you are not 100 per cent on top of your game in international cricket, you get punished, and maybe we had relaxed a bit after the Twenty20 games, not consciously, but perhaps just enough for it to be costly at the highest level. Straight after the game, when emotions are still raw and the adrenalin is still flowing, can be a touchy time to hold inquests, but it needed to be done. Peter was very forthright, as was Paul Collingwood, and I think we played better cricket afterwards as a result.

Much improved, we won in Auckland and then took part in one of the most dramatic one-day games in recent years in Napier. On a belter of a wicket, we scored 342 and then saw New Zealand equal it in a tied match. My form had been patchy but I had been batting well at Hamilton before rain came and affected our momentum and then Ravi Bopara ran me out. In Napier Phil Mustard and I really came off as an opening partnership.

We should have put on more than we did, actually, and once the Colonel was out, I should have gone on to bat through the innings, so to get out immediately after him to Ryder was disappointing. Even so, our batsmen scored runs all the way down the order, with Paul Collingwood contributing one of the quickest half centuries in English one-day international history, repeatedly chipping sixes over the short midwicket boundary, a hit of no more than 60 yards being enough to register a maximum.

In the end, after 678 runs had been scored during the day, it came down to New Zealand needing just seven runs off the last over, and Colly threw the ball to Luke Wright for his first over of the match. It was, by any standards, a real test of temperament and ability but Luke came through with flying colours to concede just six runs and the match was tied, although Colly almost executed a run-out to win us the game off the final ball.

It was a good piece of captaincy by Colly. On such a surface, we needed wickets early on, even with such a formidable score already on the board, so he decided to bowl out our best bowlers. At one point, I said to the captain that I felt Luke should be bowling earlier and that we should be keeping Sidebottom up our sleeves for later, but Colly said, 'No, the best bowlers have to bowl,' and he was quite right. It was a good lesson for me. You have to remember which bowlers the opposition would like to face least at any given time.

The run feast of Napier, when we so nearly squared the series, was followed by a rain-affected defeat in Christchurch and a 3–1 series deficit for us. Maybe we underestimated New Zealand after the two Twenty20 victories, something you should never do with them, and we were reminded that they remain the most resilient and competitive bunch of cricketers.

We had to remember that lesson for the three-Test series, because there was no doubt in my mind that we had to beat New Zealand. Okay, they had a better one-day ranking than us, but we were the better Test side, and we had to prove it after consecutive series defeats against India and Sri Lanka. There could be no excuses if we failed to beat New Zealand. It was imperative. But it was very much touch and go after a most unexpected and unwelcome First Test defeat in Hamilton, which was rapidly becoming our least favourite venue in New Zealand.

This was an eventful match, featuring some outstanding fielding from us, which I am happy to report included one of the best catches I have ever taken, and a hat-trick for Ryan Sidebottom, but also some very disappointing England batting. New Zealand may have made a decent first innings score but we were over-cautious in reply. Yes, there had been talk about us not making 400 in a first innings for a while and a need for more application in our batting, but that wasn't discussed in the dressing room. Our retreat into our shell was not a conscious thing, it just seemed to happen.

A lot of credit needs to be given to the Kiwi bowlers. Our feeling before the series was that the Kiwis wouldn't have the bowling unit to bowl us out consistently, and that they didn't do enough with the ball. What they did have was an attack that never bowled bad balls. They were just so accurate and that created its own pressure. Jacob Oram was probably the most economical bowler in world cricket while Kyle Mills and Chris Martin both hung the ball back. It was a great gameplan which they had the patience to carry out.

Our fielding, though, was a definite plus. We have done an awful lot of work on our fielding since Peter Moores became coach, and in this game everything stuck. It was a big improvement on our displays in Sri Lanka, where it seemed at times that we needed to take 24 or 25 wickets to win a match, and it's hard enough taking 20 without giving yourselves extra work to do. For me it was nice to know that the work I had done on my fielding had paid off. My fielding was something of an issue in the early stages of my career, so it was satisfying to show that I wasn't that bad after all. Everyone drops catches but if you keep working at it, you give yourself the opportunity to catch a lot more than you drop, and that is the minimum expected of any fielder at the highest level these days.

Sidebottom's hat-trick in the second innings gave us a bit of hope, false hope as it turned out, because it left us with a target just short of 300 on the final day after an attacking declaration from Daniel Vettori. We felt we would have a chance if we kept wickets in hand but I'm afraid they pretty much blew us away. We were comprehensively and fairly beaten.

This, now, was an anxious time for us. We had lost the one-day series and we had lost the first Test of a series that we just had to win. We knew the knives were out for us, as simple as that, but fortunately the Second Test in Wellington followed on rapidly and we were able to get back into action straightaway. If we didn't turn this around, it might not be exaggerating to say that jobs would be lost, but we couldn't dwell on that. We just had to go out there, dispel the dark clouds and prove the doubters wrong.

Before the match, came the announcement of one of the bravest, some might say ruthless, selection decisions that I have encountered. Steve Harmison had been struggling with his bowling and was felt to be under threat for his place, but Matthew Hoggard was also left out, and Jimmy Anderson and Stuart Broad brought in. Hoggy, in particular, seemed very despondent because there was an argument that the batsmen had been more responsible for our defeat in Hamilton than the bowlers. I think it provided everyone with a bit of a jolt. It showed that in this new era for England, nobody's place could ever be taken for granted, and it sent a message to us all that we should never be surprised if we are left out after a few bad games. The hard option was something that the new regime were not afraid to take.

But however much sympathy you have for team-mates and friends when they are dropped, the validity of any decision can only be judged by results and, in this instance, the move by Michael Vaughan, Peter Moores or whoever it was who decided to drop the two Ashes heroes, proved absolutely right.

There was no huge meeting this time, nothing like the one we had after the one-day defeat in Hamilton. We just felt we had been too timid against the bowling of Vettori and allowed their other bowlers to dictate to us. We had to go out and play with the confidence we know we can display, and that is what we did, even though at one stage, the match hung in the balance. If it hadn't been for the sixth-wicket stand between Paul Collingwood and Tim Ambrose, and our new wicketkeeper's subsequent century, we could easily have gone two down and lost the series. And the implications of that do not bear thinking about.

If ever there is a man for a crisis situation it's Colly, while Ambrose showed the strength of character to score a hundred in only his second Test after replacing Matt Prior, and that augurs well for his international future. Together they rescued England. Tim survived a testing over from Jacob Oram at the end of the first day, which left him waiting for three figures until the morning.

Tim is quite a rounded, laid-back character, one of those guys who's good at everything he turns his hand to. He's an excellent guitarist, but quite shy about his musical ability, unlike Graeme Swann who is the archetypal front man in any England musical gathering.

That most crucial of wins in Wellington, which also featured an excellent bowling performance from Jimmy Anderson on his return to the side, set up a winner takes all

Third and final Test back in Napier, where again we had to recover from a position of some trouble. On a terrible first morning, we crashed to four for three and needed a rescue act just as dramatic as the one provided by Ambrose and Collingwood in the Second Test. It came initially from Kevin Pietersen. Kev had been having a quiet run by his standards but truly great players do not stay quiet for long, and Pietersen is one of them. KP and Stuart Broad lifted us to 280 in our first innings and, after that, the Test went perfectly for us. Stuart's mature batting contribution showed he has the ability to become a genuine all-rounder.

The match went especially well for Andrew Strauss. One of England's most experienced players, and an England captain less than two years earlier, Andrew was under a lot of pressure as he emerged for his second innings on a pair in that deciding Test. He had been left out of the squad to tour Sri Lanka but returned at the expense of the unfortunate Ravi Bopara, and hadn't got too many runs ahead of that last innings of the tour. Now it was being widely speculated that this might be his last chance, but what character and what ability the man showed to score 170 and put us firmly on the path to victory. I can only imagine what Andrew would have been thinking ahead of that innings. One thing it showed was that you're never far away from being in nick if you're a quality player.

That match provided another example of us bouncing back, and showed that we were resilient when the pressure was on. Okay, we realize that we might not be able to get away with escape acts against the very best teams in the world, and we will have to start dominating games from the front if we are to become the best, but battling back in adversity is not a bad quality to have.

New Zealand never lay down and die, and even though we set them 470 to win, some big hitting from Tim Southee kept us waiting for what was still a comprehensive end to the series. All it did was delay our drinking time, because then followed a great night in one of the bars in Napier, where we were joined by a big contingent of the Barmy Army, who had supported us in huge numbers throughout the tour. Voices of dissent may have been raised when we struggled in Sri Lanka, but this was far more typical of our amazing following – great support and a good night in the bar, players mixing with well-wishers in the happiest of circumstances.

I love the Barmy Army. I think when I come to the end of my career, I will remember the encouragement they give us as much as anything. They are usually fairly quiet in the first session of a day's play, often sleeping off the excesses of the night before, but they start to warm up after lunch and are usually in good voice after tea.

It sends shivers down your spine when they sing 'Jerusalem' or my song, and I would like to put on record my immense gratitude to them for all their support.

It is fair to say that we were not necessarily at our best for much of the New Zealand tour but, to a large extent, as long as you win, that's all that matters. Yes, there is always room for improvement but after two losing Test series and then going one down, having lost the one-day series, we had to be satisfied with a 2–1 victory. We would have plenty of other opportunities to show what we could do against New Zealand because they were going to be our first opponents in our 2008 summer.

14

FAMILIARITY BREEDS SUCCESS

Facing New Zealand at home in the early part of 2008, immediately after beating them away, was a bit like playing the DVD of a film that you enjoy over and over again. Familiarity did not exactly breed contempt but it bred success from our point of view as we were able to complete our second successive series win over the Black Caps.

The continued suggestion, particularly in the media, that New Zealand were not an especially good side, and so we should be beating them convincingly, never persuaded me that was the case. For a start, the Kiwis are an extremely accomplished one-day side and, to me, good cricketers are good cricketers at any kind of cricket, and if they are good for 50 overs, they cannot be too bad over the longer distance.

Okay, their results at Test level are not as good as they are in one-dayers, but we found them extremely competent opponents, and by the end of our near six-month battle we were pleased to have got them out of the way with two Test series won. New Zealand don't seem to get the credit they deserve. They are a good unit and certainly get the best out of themselves.

Ahead of their arrival, we talked long and hard about the need to keep winning series, to get into good habits and to build momentum. It had not escaped our notice that the build-up to the successful Ashes series of 2005 had started with victory over New Zealand at home, and that was something we needed to repeat now.

The First Test at Lord's was not a typical match at headquarters. We certainly fancied our chances of winning after taking a first-innings lead and having New Zealand in a bit of trouble second time round, but in the end it was a question of the weather having the final word. With a fair bit of early season rain around, there was not enough time to force a positive result. We were the only side who could have won over the last four or five sessions but it would not have been a certain England victory if the game had gone the full distance.

The weather had been horrible in the build-up to the game so we had no hesitation in bowling when we won the toss, and we would have dismissed New Zealand very cheaply if it had not been for Brendon McCullum, who batted really well. We had seen enough of McCullum in New Zealand to realize that he has become a seriously good player and great competitor, and he fell three short of a hundred here as New Zealand reached 277, with Ryan Sidebottom, our best bowler, taking four wickets.

This match marked the return of the Cook–Strauss opening partnership, since Michael Vaughan had decided that he would prefer to return to number three in the order, which was absolutely his prerogative, and understandable, because he had so much on his mind as captain. It was a shame, though, in some ways – we were working well together as openers, and had scored runs. We are such different players that the bowlers are constantly forced to change their thinking and their line of attack, but for the good of himself and the team the captain felt we needed a change. A captain has every right to choose where he bats because it is not easy to open after you have just spent 120 overs directing operations in the field.

It was said that Andrew and I are too similar as players to be a potent partnership and I can see that point of view. In a perfect world you would like a left-hand/right-hand combination and we are both left-handers with certain technical similarities. But I did not accept that we could not function together, because we had already done so as a second-wicket partnership, and we could do so again. When we had opened together previously, Andrew had had a bit of a bad run, but he had returned in some style in the final Test in New Zealand in Napier and we were looking forward to joining forces at the top of the order again.

So it was good to debunk, at an early stage, any suggestion that we could not play well together with a century partnership as we replied with 319 to take a first-innings lead. My innings, though, was cut short on 61, the start, as it transpired, of a run of scores above 50 but below a hundred. The truth of the matter was that this was the start of a run when I was not happy with my form. You have times in your career when you are not entirely fluent and when you have slight technical issues that you have to address, and for some reason the 2008 season started to unravel for me. I just didn't feel 100 per cent right.

It was hardly a crisis because the half centuries were still coming, but I will never be totally satisfied with my own form unless I'm scoring hundreds, and the 2008 season became a matter of me working on my balance at the crease.

The main man at Lord's, however, was our captain. Vaughan scored one of those hundreds that reminds you what a fantastic player he is, as good as any batsman in the world. He was under pressure, as he always seemed to be – wrongly, in my view – and the fact that we were playing New Zealand again, and the weather wasn't great, meant that the buzz wasn't quite as good as it normally is in a Lord's Test. But Vaughan always seems to score runs when he and the England cricket team need them most, and that is a very valuable knack to have. On this occasion, it was the best memory for England to take from a fairly low-key start to the international season.

The Second Test, at Old Trafford, turned into a massive test of character for the England team. We had to show our mettle on one of the grounds where we have been most successful in recent years. A defeat would have been calamitous in a series that we really had to win, but the fact that we avoided it spoke volumes about our reserves of strength.

The match started with a fantastic innings from Ross Taylor, which showed what a good player he has become for New Zealand. Taylor started off as a one-day player and, in a sign of the times, played some shots that just wouldn't have been seen in Test cricket ten years ago. He is certainly becoming a formidable opponent. Taylor's unbeaten 154 guided the tourists to 381 after they had won the toss, and they strengthened that good position when they bowled us out for 202 with only Andrew Strauss scoring runs in our first innings.

Daniel Vettori bowled excellently, sending down some really testing variations, and we only just avoided the follow-on, which was a desperate situation to be in. England were in trouble, no question about that. New Zealand had the sort of lead that any side should be able to take on to clinch victory, particularly on a wicket that traditionally takes more spin as the game progresses.

Michael Vaughan's message to us was simple. He said, 'It's up to us now. It's up to these eleven people to get us out of this. If we don't do it, then we're going to be in for hell.' The captain remained calm. Vaughan is extremely good in those circumstances. He never panics, never over-reacts, and his words were just what we needed to hear. He remained authoritative and emphasized to us that if we bowled well, the Black Caps could easily collapse.

I remember New Zealand going into a huddle at the end of our innings. Apparently, Vettori said to his players that if they batted well, they would win the game, but it looked to me as though they thought the game was already done and dusted, and with a big lead and bowling last, especially with Vettori in their ranks, all they had to do was turn up. Certainly the Kiwis batted as though they thought the match was won. Monty Panesar was getting the ball to lift and bounce and hit them on the chest and arm but they were insistent on playing big shots against him as if they already had enough runs.

Monty was brilliant. He really is a match-winner when conditions suit him, which they always seem to do at Old Trafford. Okay, at this stage of his career he might not have as many variations as Vettori, if you want to compare the two left-arm spinners, but on this occasion the younger and less experienced man indisputably came out on top. Panesar took six for 37, New Zealand were dismissed for 114, and from the most precarious of positions we were suddenly right back in the game.

Panesar has the ability to bowl quicker than most spinners and still deliver that all-important flight. It gives the batsman just that little bit less time to think about things and Monty's stock ball is always hard to handle. His challenge is to become a better bowler in one-day cricket by adding more variations of pace and angles, as Vettori does, and I'm sure that will come in time. I think he has the potential to be England's best-ever spinner.

Now we were in with a chance, but it was still not going to be easy. We had to chase 294 to win and anything close to 300 is never straightforward in Test cricket. New Zealand remained the favourites but we had chased that sort of total before and we were confident we could do so again.

I cursed myself for getting out for 28 before the close of the third day and, at 76 for one going into the fourth, the match was very much in the balance, but Andrew Strauss, now fully restored as a prolific member of the England batting line-up, scored a century that was quite unbelievable in the conditions, to set us on course for our target.

There had been some talk about the pace at which we were

scoring our runs but our tempo was perfect here and Strauss was at the centre of that, together with an important contribution from Vaughan. Kevin Pietersen also chipped in before Ian Bell and Paul Collingwood, the two batsmen who were perceived to be under pressure, saw us home to a six-wicket victory. We had dug ourselves into a hole but we had dug ourselves out of it again, and everybody had played their part in that.

The fact that Ian's place was under threat seemed particularly strange to me. He had scored a hundred just two matches earlier but after missing once, the spotlight was turned on him. I guess it's the way the media works and once a player gets a score they move on to the next one. We would rather have won from the front, of course, but it was a brilliant fightback and that gave us a lot of confidence going into the final match of the series at Trent Bridge.

I can understand why a lot of people think it is a shame that we will not be playing Australia at Old Trafford in 2009, nor indeed playing Test cricket there at all for another couple of years. It's certainly a wicket that Monty would like to wrap up and carry around with him. We really should utilize every bit of home advantage we can get.

It's the same with the Barmy Army. I think it's a great shame that we do not really see them as a group at home Test matches. They give us such a lift at away games. If you are having a tough day and you hear the trumpeter strike up after tea, it can really help. They give you that bit of extra pride and can put a spring in your step. Away from home they can completely take over grounds but at home it seems as though they are not really encouraged to sit together. That's a pity. Surely a group of seats at each ground could be sold *en bloc* to the Barmy Army. It would be great, and at a time when Test cricket could well be coming under threat from the rise and rise of Twenty20 cricket anything that encourages a great atmosphere and people to come to the games can only be good.

Anyway, it's not for me to question where we play home Test matches and I am sure there are sound reasons for us not playing at Old Trafford, whether it is to do with the redevelopment of the ground, or money earned, but the England team do seem to play well there and it does seem to be a ground that produces attractive cricket.

At Trent Bridge, England's performance was much more emphatic. We didn't start too well, admittedly, after being sent in first, but thanks to a hundred from Kevin Pietersen and good contributions from Tim Ambrose and Stuart Broad we got up to 364 and never looked back.

Then it was over to Jimmy Anderson. I have said before that he is my best mate in the team so I feel I can say that Jimmy knows he hasn't always been consistent enough for England. But he has always had the ability to be a wicket-taker at the highest level in the right conditions and now we saw him swing the ball around corners on a ground that has become synonymous with the art.

Jimmy had his first proper run in the England team in 2008, something that had been denied him in the past mainly because of injury but also due to that inconsistency. Now at Trent Bridge he charged in and took the first six wickets.

For a while it looked as if he might be on course to take all ten in the innings, something that no England bowler has done since Jim Laker took 19 wickets in a match, against Australia at Old Trafford in 1956.

In those circumstances, someone else usually pops up to get a wicket, which is what Ryan Sidebottom did here, but Anderson was magnificent to finish with seven for 43 as New Zealand were bundled out for 123 and were quickly following on. They showed a bit more resistance in the second innings but thanks to Ryan Sidebottom's six-wicket haul the game was quickly finished off on the Sunday morning and we were able to relish a 2–0 series victory and a job well done. You really have to savour moments like that.

I think another difference with Jimmy now is that, when he's batting, he doesn't go for runs if conditions are not in his favour, something that has added to his armoury. There is no reason why he should not become a formidable, consistent performer for England, and I would be delighted if he does.

England, meanwhile, had two consecutive series wins over New Zealand. We were the favourites both times, but that can bring its own pressures, and it should be remembered that not too many sides win in New Zealand. The same side had played five successive Test matches and that continuity was good for the team. While understanding that the England cricket team is by no means a closed shop, the unity and familiarity engendered by that consistency of selection undoubtedly helped our overall performances.

Another one-day series beckoned but for me there was the

disappointment of picking up an injury that was to rule me out of most of the 50-over matches against New Zealand. I think I hurt my shoulder on the Saturday of the Trent Bridge Test. It was basically an impingement of my right shoulder, which is something I'd had before and I thought would be cured by an injection. I was pretty sure that I would quickly be able to resume but every time I picked up a bat I felt a sharp pain in my shoulder. Three injections later – two steroidal and one anti-inflammatory – I was finally ready to play.

It was the first time that I had missed England matches through injury and it was very frustrating. Forced on to the sidelines, you become bored, impatient and concerned that you might lose your place, so you spend your time searching for any little indication that you are ready to return. I just had to put up with it.

I missed the Twenty20 game against New Zealand, which we won emphatically, and was ruled out of the first one-day international at Chester-le-Street, which became notable for a remarkable piece of innovation from Kevin Pietersen. Kevin had caused a stir when he had reverse swept Muttiah Muralitharan for six in the Test at Edgbaston in 2006 but now he surpassed himself. Pietersen not once but twice changed his stance, switching to a left-handed position and grip to hit medium-paced balls from Scott Styris for six both times, the first over mid-wicket and the second, even more remarkably, over long-on. The second one was a slower ball, too. Kev just waited for it and hit it out of the ground.

I don't know how he does it. I don't think anyone else in

the world could have played those shots. It was extraordinary cricket that everyone present that day will always remember, yet there were still gripes about it. Some members of the bowlers union said the shots should be outlawed because the batsman was not giving the bowler notice that he was going to bat left-handed. I don't see that argument. Firstly, the shots were wonderful entertainment, and secondly, I imagine most bowlers worth their salt would be perfectly happy if an opponent decided to bat left-handed because surely it gives the bowler a better chance of getting the batsman out.

Anyway, Kevin's switch hitting was part of a pretty perfect one-day performance. Following on from the Test and Twenty20 victories, it seemed to set us up for a good limited-overs series but, as I've said, New Zealand have a formidable one-day side that must never be underestimated, and they hit back in an emphatic manner.

The weather-affected game at Edgbaston was eventually declared to have no result, and was contentious because we were accused of delaying tactics, taking the regular break between innings when New Zealand wanted to get after the 165 they needed for victory, under Duckworth-Lewis rules. Well, the first thing to say is that New Zealand would have done exactly the same as us in our position. They were not certain to win, anyway, and you just don't hand victories to the opposition at international level. The stakes are too high. But I would certainly agree that, in a shortened game, a half-hour gap is too long, and that was duly changed in time for the next game.

Bristol was a missed opportunity for us, but as I wasn't there to see the low-scoring game it's hard for me to pinpoint where we went wrong. Then came the match at The Oval, which was, shall we say, slightly eventful. People say that the 50-over game might be dying but this was gripping, full of drama, a great game of cricket that went right down to the wire.

Yet what it will be remembered for is the run-out of Grant Elliott, which led to all sorts of problems for our captain, Paul Collingwood. Trouble flared when Elliott, in attempting a quick run, collided with Ryan Sidebottom and was left stranded on the ground as Kevin Pietersen took off the bails. Umpire Mark Benson asked our captain if he wanted to proceed with an appeal, Colly thought about it and decided he would. Then the question arose, was it in the spirit of the game?

I wasn't playing but I was there when it was all going off and the first thing to say is that I felt extremely sorry for Paul Collingwood. He was faced with having to make a tough decision. Okay, I think he got it wrong, but it was an extremely difficult situation and I certainly didn't think the incident merited the uproar that followed. Paul made a mistake but he apologized for it and that should have been the end of the matter.

It took a big man to go into the New Zealand dressing room after the game with tensions still running high, and Colly already aware that he'd slipped up, but they were then in the wrong not to shake his hand, in my opinion, something for which I think Daniel Vettori later apologized himself. In a way, I think that was worse than what Colly did, especially as they had won the game. Whatever happens on the pitch should stay on the pitch and teams should always put it behind them afterwards, shake hands and move on. Yes, I think Paul made a mistake, and he agreed, but not everybody in our camp thought he was at fault, so let's not just assume he had messed up. It wasn't totally black and white and it was a heated situation. No one can be totally sure of what he would have done in those circumstances. Possibly someone in the team could have advised Colly but it comes down to what the captain wants to do. If he has eight or nine people in his ear all giving their opinion, it can only add to the sense of confusion. I'm glad it wasn't me making that decision, that's for sure.

It was a bad day for Paul Collingwood's career and one that got immediately worse when he was suspended for four matches for our poor over rate in that game. That led to Kevin Pietersen being put in charge for the final match of the series at Lord's, the first that I played, and he conducted himself very well. In truth, most people can put tactics into operation in the field, and captaincy has to encompass the complete package. Kevin did all that could be expected of him as a stand-in but unfortunately we didn't chase well and lost both the game and the series.

After the one-day wins against India at home and Sri Lanka away, we had lost two series on the bounce against New Zealand, our ups and downs in one-day cricket continuing. But the Tests had been won and we now moved on to face the challenge of South Africa, knowing that they would provide formidable opposition for us in the second half of the 2008 domestic summer.

15

GOODBYE TO OUR ASHES WINNING CAPTAIN

We went into our last Test series of the 2008 summer full of optimism that we would be able to defeat South Africa and prove ourselves as the second best Test team in the world. Unfortunately, in a series full of drama, good cricket and controversy, we ended up losing not just the series but our highly respected captain Michael Vaughan. It was a sad and emotional time.

Everything started well enough. We seemed to be thought of as underdogs by most people and there was much talk about South Africa's pace attack, not least by the South Africans themselves, which put a little pressure on their players to deliver the goods. South Africa went into the First Test at Lord's with everybody expecting great things from Dale Steyn, Morne Morkel and the rest, but England made all the running, at least for the first three days. We played some top-quality cricket, our best for a while, based around two superlative centuries. A first-innings score in excess of 400, achieved for the first time for 13 Tests, put us in a wonderful position to take a 1–0 lead in this four-match series.

Andrew Strauss and I got off to a good start but my penchant for getting to 60 and not going on struck again.

Then Kevin Pietersen was simply magnificent to put us in the driving seat with a big century on his first Test appearance against South Africa. Kev had made an immediate impact against the country of his birth when he played in the one-day series in South Africa at the start of his England career in 2005 and now he was doing it again in spectacular fashion. He was almost guaranteed to score a hundred in this match, it seemed to be part of the script!

Yet even Pietersen's 152 was overshadowed by an incredible effort from Ian Bell. He played the innings of his life, an innings that not many people could play. By the time he reached 199 he had shown what a supremely gifted batsman he is and, with a score of 593 for eight declared, we could not lose the match. In fact, we were in with a very good chance of winning it, and that possibility was considerably enhanced when we bowled South Africa out for 247 and made them follow on, Monty Panesar taking four wickets.

That was when the series started to become a lot tougher for us. Sri Lanka had managed to bat themselves to a draw at Lord's in 2006 after following on but we had dropped a few catches in that match and this time our hopes were high that we could force through our advantage and take a hard-earned lead. But perhaps we had not appreciated just how good this Lord's wicket was. It remained so flat on days four and five that it was almost impossible to achieve a break through. As I've said, Lord's is a special place to play cricket, but maybe the wickets are becoming a little too conducive to draws. I don't think there has been a positive result at Lord's since 2005. Maybe as a batsman I shouldn't complain but in this Twenty20 age the great game of Test cricket needs to ensure that it remains the pinnacle and the form that the spectators most want to see. An international match should start with flat wickets but the surface should be deteriorating by day four. Then the skill of the spin bowlers becomes an increasing factor in the outcome.

Our bowlers threw everything at South Africa in their second innings and could not have done anything more, but the tourists were able to bat out six sessions. South Africa moved along to 393 for the loss of only three wickets, two of them falling to Jimmy Anderson, and we just had to accept the inevitability of the draw.

That match took its toll. We reported for the Second Test at Headingley the following week with injury worries over firstly Ryan Sidebottom and then, at a late stage on the day before the match, Jimmy Anderson. I think the strain of bowling so many overs at Lord's, added to the demanding workload on any regular international bowler, caused them both to be unsure about whether they would be ready to play another Test so soon after the last one. The uncertainty over their fitness led to a major controversy when Darren Pattinson joined us. His inclusion in the England team for his Test debut almost became a cause for national debate.

It started off innocuously enough. When it became clear to the powers that be that Sidebottom in particular was struggling to shake off his niggles in time to play, it was felt that another swing bowler would be needed to supplement our squad. Step forward a man born in Grimsby who had spent most of his life in Melbourne and who had been making a considerable impression on his debut season in English cricket with Nottinghamshire. No one in the team had a problem with that. It was always going to be hard for him, coming into the England set-up when he barely knew anybody. He had not had the chance to practise with us the day before the game, or even to meet us at the hotel, but it is unfair to say he had a detrimental affect on us.

I could understand what Michael Vaughan meant when he said afterwards that the selection had caused a bit of disturbance to the team but that would have been the case whoever had been brought in at the last minute to replace Sidebottom. Ryan had played such a big part for England over the previous year. Also, we had just broken a record by fielding the same side for six successive Tests and ending that run was bound to be disruptive. The flip side was that we welcomed back Andrew Flintoff for his first Test in 18 months, which was a wonderful boost to everybody after all the injury problems that Freddie has had. He is such a great character to have around and any England side is better for his presence.

Darren certainly did not bowl badly and he was not the reason we lost the Second Test. That was more down to the fact that we batted poorly on the first day, having lost the toss and been put in first because conditions suited bowling. A first-innings score of 203 was just not good enough. I think 300 in the conditions would have been par but we fell significantly short of that and were playing catch up from that moment onwards. We had also seen what all the fuss was about over Steyn and Morkel, both of whom took four wickets and bowled well.

In a controversial moment, AB De Villiers claimed a catch off Andrew Strauss when the ball appeared to touch the ground. Andrew was ruled out by the third umpire. That turned up the temperature a bit and there was an incident during South Africa's innings, when Hashim Amla spooned one towards mid-off where Michael Vaughan took what we thought was a brilliant diving catch. However, it was so low that Michael said to the umpires he wasn't entirely sure it had carried, even though to the naked eye it looked a perfectly clean catch. It was referred and, since TV cameras provide a two-dimensional image of catches, some doubt was registered and the catch was ruled out.

Couple of things to say here. Firstly, I think it was unfortunate that the catches were lumped together as being in the same category when De Villiers' effort clearly wasn't a catch and Michael's almost certainly was. Then there is the whole question of the technology. We seem to be getting into these situations all too often with catches and I just think it is a shame that, in this day and age, the cameras are not available to provide three-dimensional images. Are they not out there somewhere? If they are, or if they can be developed, we will go a long way towards ending the controversy over incidents such as these two.

Michael's ruled-out catch was a crucial moment at Headingley because we would have had them under pressure if Amla had fallen at that stage. As it was, two top-class hundreds from Ashwell Prince and De Villiers began to put the game out of our reach and South Africa piled up 522, too much for us to chase successfully. We actually batted pretty well in our second innings but the damage was done and we ended up losing by ten wickets.

So we were one down in a series we desperately wanted to win with everything to do in the Third Test at Edgbaston. But this match proved to be the end of an era. After it, England's most successful ever captain decided that the time had come for another man to take the helm. It could have been so different, and would have been if we had scored more runs in our first innings, as we should have done, or successfully defended 280 in the last innings, as we could well have done.

The margins are small in sport and I have little doubt that Michael would still be in charge now if we had managed to win that game. Yes, it became clear in his emotional, dignified departing press conference that he was convinced the time had come for him to resign, but I'm sure a victory over South Africa would have had a rejuvenating effect on him, at least for a while. It was a dreadful shame that he should have gone out on such a low note, and we players have to hold up our hands and take responsibility for it. We weren't good enough at Edgbaston and the South Africans beat us fair and square.

Again, we did not score enough runs in our first innings, and this time there was little excuse because conditions were not as favourable for bowling as they were in Leeds. I got beyond the sixties but fell in the seventies to an old friend from Essex, which made it even worse – not that you would have thought Andre Nel was a friend, judging by his animated behaviour. I had wondered whether Nel, one of the more aggressive bowlers in world cricket, would go through his whole sledging, theatrical repertoire towards me, because we were close when he was a very popular member of our side at Chelmsford. I should not have been surprised when he was louder towards me than he was towards anyone else. I enjoyed the battle!

Nelly has an alter-ego when he steps on to the field, a character called Gunter, a mad German from the mountains starved of air, or so he likes to tell people. Having come into the side as a replacement for the injured Dale Steyn, Andre had told the world about his pal Gunter in a pre-match press conference so that everyone could watch out for him. I was determined not to engage with him and just let him huff and puff and get himself more frustrated, which is what he did until he got me with a good one and gave me a send-off. No doubt he will remind me of that if he comes back to Essex. I really hope he does.

Flintoff got us back into the match with some fantastic fast bowling to Jacques Kallis, which provided an intense, gripping passage of Test cricket that advertised the longer game at its very best. Thanks to Fred and the other bowlers, we restricted South Africa's lead to a lot less than once we feared, and when Kevin Pietersen and Paul Collingwood produced an excellent stand in our second innings, we really did think we were about to level the series.

Before Colly went out to bat, someone in our dressing room said that if he scored a hundred now, it would be one of the best ever played because Paul was under so much pressure after continuing his run of low scores in the first innings – and he hit a century full of more character and defiance than I have ever seen. It gave us that lead of 280, which should have been enough. But Graeme Smith produced an innings that usurped even Colly's to take South Africa to a five-wicket victory late on the fourth day. The series was gone.

The defeat hit us hard and on that Saturday night I had the feeling that something was up. It was horribly disappointing. I know fairytale endings are rare but Michael Vaughan deserved better than that. I saw the captain on the Sunday morning, when it had become apparent that he was going, and I wished him well. I felt for him. Chatting about the cricket he was fine, but as soon as he mentioned his family you could see how much it had affected him. It was a sad, sad day.

The one positive for Vaughan is that stepping down should free him up as a batsman. He was averaging 50 as a Test player before becoming captain, which is phenomenal. When you take away the responsibilities of the job, with all its meetings and media conferences, I am sure that will have a beneficial effect on his game. It might not happen straight away but I'm convinced he will score runs. He is too good a player not to.

When the news broke, I must admit it did cross my mind that I might be a candidate to succeed him. As I've said, being an England player in itself provides enough challenges without getting too far ahead of yourself, and being captain is not something I've wasted much effort thinking about, but I did wonder whether this might be my time. I have been around for a while now, and I play in both the Test and one-day international sides. The selectors wanted the same captain for both forms of the game once it became clear that Paul Collingwood, too, was going to stand down.

It was only a fleeting thought, though. To be honest, I realized it would have been too early for me. The obvious choice was Kevin Pietersen and he was duly handed the captaincy two days after our defeat at Edgbaston. Kev has the credentials and will do the job confidently and in his own way. He has dealt with everything thrown at him so far in his career and has done unbelievably well. I'm sure the challenge will only inspire him to greater things.

The challenge for us was to forget what went before and find some form under a new leader. KP is a strong-minded individual and you need that because captaining England is a hard job. The media interest is bigger than ever and the Twenty20 explosion brings extra challenges with it. But it's also a massively rewarding job when you lead your country to victory. Maybe one day it really will be my time. Who knows?

Now we had to provide a strong showing in the final Test at The Oval, both as a tribute to Vaughan and also to get the Kevin Pietersen era off to the best possible start. Kev was very positive when he talked to us about his expectations, and he sent us all a text message the night before the game, wishing us good luck and telling us to enjoy it. One of the statements of intent KP made the day before the match was to tell Steve Harmison that not only would he be returning to the side but he would be taking the new ball for England for the first time in a year.

We had hoped that we would be batting first but, in fact, the loss of the toss proved to be something of a blessing because our bowlers performed with pace, hostility and accuracy to dispatch South Africa for 194 in arguably our best day of the series since Lord's. It could have been the most perfect of starts had I been able to cling on to a chance in the gully off Harmison off the very first ball. Graeme Smith slashed hard and I was unable to hold it, which was highly frustrating for me after the improvements I have made to my fielding. It could have been the perfect start for KP as skipper!

I managed to hold a catch later in the innings but unfortunately dropped another, so it was some relief to me that we bowled South Africa out cheaply. All I can say about my catching is that I believe it was just one of those things and I will endeavour to hold on to far more than I drop in future.

When we batted, I was determined to end my run without a three-figure score but didn't manage it. High-scoring honours went to our new captain. He made a hundred in his first match as Test captain with some fantastic strokemaking, and his contribution, along with some great late-order hitting from Harmison, ensured that we gained a healthy lead of 122.

For a long time it looked as though that lead, despite a miserable Saturday shortened by rain, would be enough to give us victory in four days, but a frustrating stand of 95 from AB De Villiers and Paul Harris left us with a challenging little target of 197 to finish the series on a high note.

And that is exactly what we did. It may not have made up for losing overall but our victory at The Oval, which was comfortable in the end, gave us some not inconsiderable consolation and something to take into our winter assignments in India and the West Indies.

There were runs again for me, too, 67 of them, but that hundred continued to prove elusive. At least I averaged nearly 50 in the series without reaching three figures, so it is not that I have been doing badly. If I carry on like this, the hundreds will come again.

16

MY TWENTY20 VISION

It was always my dream to play for England as a youngster and to sit here now, at the age of 24, having done so more than 30 times in Test cricket, as well as in one-day cricket, is amazing. I'm very proud of what I have achieved so far. But it's never enough, is it? It's human nature, I think, never to be satisfied, although if it all ended here and I never played for my country again, I would be extremely happy with what I have done. I have had the opportunity to represent my country and that is something I will always cherish, whatever lies ahead.

As a young batsman, I could not have asked for much more in my first two and a half years of international cricket, but people talk about batsmen peaking at around 30 years of age, so I have some way to go yet with, I hope, plenty of challenges to face. Whenever a Test match hundred comes along, I'll prize it as much as any that have gone before because they do not come along that often, even though the first few came along quite quickly for me.

How good can I be as an England cricketer? That is a difficult question to answer but I hope to be quite a bit better than I am now. I'm not the type of person to shout from the rooftops about what I intend to do but I know what my cricketing goals are. It's a bit strange to be thinking about the end of my career, but I am confident that I will be able to look back when it all ends, satisfied that I did all that I possibly could to be a success. In ten years' time I will know whether my goals have been achieved.

Am I a better player now than when I first played for England in early 2006? Well, I certainly think my game has improved against spin because the forward press method that Duncan Fletcher taught me has benefited me hugely. When I look back on my hundred on debut in Nagpur, I can see that a few bat/pad chances sort of flitted away to safety and I hope I would not be offering them now. I rode my luck in that innings but I feel more confident about my game now because of the general experience gained from playing 30-odd Tests and scoring more than 2,000 Test runs. Just being around the England set-up makes you a better player.

I'm not going to state specific targets because that would be setting them up to be shot down, but I can say that I have a certain number of Test runs in mind, and if someone offered them to me now, I would shake his hand and accept. I have targets, boxes to tick, as I have mentioned throughout this book, but it's a case of steady as you go.

How has my life changed since I started playing for England? Not an awful lot, really. I'm recognized a bit more by the public and if there are autograph-signing sessions at games, I have a much longer queue than I used to have. When I started, people were more concerned about getting Darren Gough's autograph at Essex but they tend to want mine now, which is nice.

I'm grateful that my life outside cricket has changed very little. I like to keep things simple away from the cricket field, and mostly spend days off relaxing as an antidote to rushing around and living the life of an international cricketer.

Have I changed? Well, you would have to ask people I knew before I played for England. You do change with getting older, of course. You grow up a bit. At 24 I'm not the same as I was when I first started playing cricket professionally at 18, but I really hope I haven't changed too much because I try my hardest to be the same person I have always been. Maybe you should ask my girlfriend, Alice, if I have changed.

Alice and I have been together for a while now and she is a huge part of my life. She is my best friend, always there for me. I know everyone says that about their partner, but she never changes whether I get a hundred or a duck and that's good. She doesn't know much about cricket, which is great because when we're together it means we don't talk about my cover drive, but she's getting more interested the more cricket she sees.

She doesn't consider herself a WAG, that's for sure. It can be so hard for wives and girlfriends when we are away from home so often. The profession is not conducive to family life but all that means is that you appreciate the support you get all the more.

We don't actually see each other as often as we'd like because, even when I'm not on the road, we don't live that close. You just have to accept it as part and parcel of the privileged life that cricketers lead. It's a tough long distance relationship but she's awesome and long may it continue.

I still keep in contact with quite a few old school friends but the people I see most often these days, quite naturally, are cricketing friends. I share a house with Mark Pettini, the Essex captain. He's a great guy and has done a great job turning the club round with Paul Grayson after Ronni Irani left. The guys at Essex have always been great to me and even though I don't spend too much time with them they remain very close friends. I am proud to be an Essex player. However much time you spend with England does not change that.

My family have been hugely supportive. As I have said, they are not the sort of people to get carried away with anything I may achieve but I like to think they are very proud and pleased for me, and I am never short of support at Test matches from those nearest to me. I hope that carries on for a long time, although it must be horrible for parents and brothers to watch you playing for England or Essex, because they cannot do anything to influence the outcome. At least, out on the field, we can try to do something to affect the course of our destiny!

The game of cricket is evolving by the day, and has certainly changed immeasurably since I first played for England. Firstly, the whole back-up system behind the England side has grown enormously, even in my brief time as an England player. It's got so much better and, together with the Professional Cricketers' Association, there is now a massive support unit underpinning the England team. That is brilliant and can only improve in the years to come.

But the biggest development to affect the game, even in my short time, is unquestionably the rise of Twenty20 cricket.

I would dearly love to look in a crystal ball to see how the whole scenario is going to pan out over the next few years.

The cricket authorities have got a difficult job on their hands. As I write, all the money in the game is going into Twenty20 cricket, this new phenomenon that seems to be taking over. I think, for instance, that Essex earn more money from one Twenty20 game than they do from the whole county championship season.

With the introduction of the Indian Premier League (IPL), and the emergence of other Twenty20 competitions, some cricketers may soon be earning more than a million pounds a year, which seems extraordinary – or maybe it isn't. In most other major sports, it causes not a murmur when the players earn vast sums – I'm thinking of football and golf – but people still seem surprised when cricketers climb into the same pay bracket. Padraig Harrington wins the Open and nobody questions the fact that he takes home three quarters of a million pounds, but cricket, up to now, has somehow been different. No one laughs or scoffs at the money earned by golfers so why should it be very different for cricketers.

Maybe it's the tradition behind cricket that makes people feel we shouldn't earn that amount of money from our game. And, in fact, is it that great? For with the emergence of Twenty20 cricket comes a very real threat to Test cricket, which hits at the very fabric of the game, especially in England, where there are plenty of traditionalists who still love the longer form of the game.

In my eyes, there is nothing better than Test-match cricket.

The Ashes series of 2005 and another great series in 2009 proved that. A game of Twenty20 cricket lasts for three hours, and often it's only the last 20 minutes that really mean something. But a game of Test cricket evolves over several days, and has so many twists, turns and nuances, providing all those gripping sub-plots to extend the drama. People will miss that if it ever goes.

You only have to look at what is happening in the cricketing world to be concerned about the way the game is changing. Sri Lanka pulled out of a proposed tour to England early in 2009 because the bulk of their players had signed to the IPL, and Chris Gayle, captain of the West Indies team who came in their place, then said he would soon give up Test cricket to concentrate on the shorter game. And, apparently, MS Dhoni, one of India's greatest players, has decided to opt out of a Test series, rather than miss any Twenty20 or one-day cricket, because he feels in need of a break – he is resting when the ultimate form of the game is going on.

It worries me that Sri Lanka's players feel they want to put the IPL ahead of a tour to England, because a tour of England must be one of the most attractive dates in any international cricketer's calendar. The first three days of any Test in England are pretty much sold out, and that remains vitally significant in the cricketing world.

Even if Test cricket seems to be safe in England, what about other countries? When we went to New Zealand early in 2008 there would have been some very empty grounds if it had not been for the thousands of travelling England supporters, and that scenario is replicated throughout the cricketing world.

So you can understand the players deciding to cash in on the Twenty20 revolution rather than grafting in Test cricket. That's where the money is and it becomes a business.

If Sri Lanka cannot send their best team to England, that is a massive worry and needs to be addressed. Okay, the International Cricket Council (ICC), the sport's governing body, have sanctioned the IPL and that's fine because it clearly is going to generate a lot of money. But if it's a properly recognized event, surely the ICC has to accommodate it by creating a window so that players can take part, and cash in on it, without jeopardizing anything else. International cricket will have to stop for those dates if administrators want the best players in the world to continue to play all forms of the game.

Now the ECB have announced that they will extend the Twenty20 Cup rather than create an English Premier League in 2010 and if England want the best players in the world to play in it, another window is going to have to be created while it takes place. And if that is as much of a success as the IPL, why should it stop there? If rich businessmen are prepared to pay the players, why shouldn't there be an Australian Cricket League and a South African one? There is already talk of an enhanced competition in Australia. It will work just as well in other countries and I'm sure it will be a brilliant success in each one. But how can you fit all these competitions in one calendar and still have the amount of international cricket that we have now? Surely something has got to give.

That's why I'm worried about the safeguarding of Test cricket. If the IPL is officially sanctioned, which it is, all the others will have to be sanctioned as well. Yes, it's brilliant that cricketers might be earning unprecedented sums, but is it going to be good for the ultimate form of the game? The extreme scenario is that Test cricket may die, and that concerns me.

Our game has always been quite amateurish, in a nice way. It's not used to the money that is descending on it, and has never needed to cope with the riches that are becoming available to the players. Millions of pounds are being piled into the game and how the game copes with that will define all our futures. Recently, an England player was able to earn around £250,000 a year and that was fantastic money. Everybody who could command those sums was very happy about it. Yet now, suddenly, players are being encouraged to earn in excess of a million pounds a year simply for playing Twenty20 cricket. These are extreme cases but Twenty20 specialists could coin it in without any concession to the longer game, and if a young cricketer has got the ability, the sky is the limit for him and who could begrudge him those possibilities?

I hope our game doesn't become totally dependent on Twenty20. I really do. I hope someone out there is working on making sure Test cricket remains the most important part of the game. I'm just not entirely sure, not with MS Dhoni opting out of a Test series and Sri Lanka pulling out of an England tour.

How will Twenty20 change the way the game is played? Well, batsmen will just have to become more expert at hitting the ball out of the ground, or they will not be getting the best contracts. So should I change the way I play? After all, I am fast becoming a bit old fashioned, a throwback to when players concentrated more on technique than clearing the ropes. Am I going to be the last of a breed, the last to play with an orthodox style? Not every change happens overnight, of course, but I have watched players such as Middlesex's 20-year-old batsman Dawid Malan smack the ball out of the ground in a Twenty20 quarter-final against Lancashire and I do wonder. He smashed it everywhere and I think it's fair to say that Twenty20 is breeding better players, more all-round, attacking players. So where does that leave us?

Well, I'm not sure I could change the way I play at this stage, but if there comes a time when Test cricket is not played so much, or is not the be all and end all, then I will have to change if I want to carry on playing. I haven't played many Twenty20 matches but if it comes to it, I will have to learn a way of playing the shortest form of the game. Yes, I would have to spend a lot of time in the nets slogging and being as inventive as I possibly can be but I could do it if necessary. It might take me three or four years to perfect a good enough method but I would get there.

But will Twenty20 go bang at some point? I don't know much about rugby but I'm told that rugby sevens was perceived as the brave new world of rugby union not so long ago, and people thought it might take over from the traditional 15-man version. Everyone loved it and it seemed that all the money in rugby would be aimed at sevens. Well, rugby sevens still has a big part to play in rugby union, but it hasn't taken over the game. It hasn't become the ultimate. It has found its niche but it hasn't become all-consuming.

Will it be the same for cricket? Will the current generation of cricketers be part of a huge revolution or will Twenty20 cricket go the way of rugby sevens and find its own niche without taking over the game? If Twenty20 is entertainment, if it is what cricket supporters want to watch, there is not an awful lot we can do about it. I hope that tradition will prevail because I still believe Test cricket is worth preserving and I think it should be safeguarded.

Don't get me wrong. I'm not saying Twenty20 cricket doesn't work. It can be brilliant and I love seeing all the kids at games. I want to see more people playing our national summer sport because it is my sport, but I would like to see the administrators policing it properly. I don't want Twenty20 to rule the cricketing world and I can see why it might. Why would cricketers go away on three or four-month Test tours when they could earn far more money concentrating on Twenty20? If cricket genuinely wants to safeguard against that, it will have to rise to the challenge. I just can't see how the governing body can give its blessing to the IPL and then not the EPL. Where is it going to stop?

I would love to look into the future and say, 'Actually, we were wrong to panic. There was no need. All Twenty20 did was bring more money into the game and enhanced its profile,' but I am not sure about that. We will just have to wait and see if Twenty20 revolutionizes the game.

It is an exciting time to be a cricketer, make no mistake about that. Burn-out was an issue not too long ago but it isn't now, not with the rewards that are on offer these days. We live in such interesting times that the concept of cricketers being too tired to take up the myriad possibilities available to them has gone out of the window.

So where will I be in ten years' time? I don't know but if I am still playing cricket, and still playing for England, I will be very happy indeed. I know one thing. I am incredibly fortunate to have done what I have done already and I am just looking forward to what comes next. Watch this space!

17

TURMOIL IN THE ENGLAND CAMP

You could say we had an eventful winter before the Ashes of 2009, the biggest series of them all. Whereas Michael Vaughan's Ashes winners of 2005 had built momentum in the eighteen months or so before defeating Australia, we had to overcome considerable adversity and not a little controversy before facing Ricky Ponting's side. Changes at the helm of the England team provided us all with the challenges that come with upheaval.

It all started, of course, with our little jaunt to Antigua for the Stanford Series, the Twenty20 challenge that turned into one of the biggest controversies in English cricket history.

The first thing to say about it is that a lot of people thought I was very lucky to be in Antigua in the first place. This was an opportunity for each England cricketer to win a million dollars. All we had to do was be selected for the side and win a game of Twenty20 cricket against Allen Stanford's West Indian Superstars.

We arrived for the match against the American billionaire's team on the back of a highly encouraging end to the 2008 season. We had won the final Test and the one-day series against South Africa under Kevin Pietersen's captaincy, and hopes were high for a winter that also included tours to India and the West Indies.

But first came this unique little trip that we were to undertake following the ECB's five-year deal with Sir Allen. I am the first to admit that, at that stage of my career, I was not one of the best fourteen Twenty20 players in England, and I guess it was only natural for some people to feel that more deserving players could have been given a shot at instant riches, unprecedented for cricketers.

I could see their point of view, but as I understand it, the England selectors wanted the 50-over squad who had just defeated South Africa to be kept together, particularly as we were to travel straight to India from Antigua for what was sure to be a hugely demanding one-day series. So I was in the squad, even though I was unlikely to play in Antigua, while Dimi Mascarenhas and Graham Napier, both of whom had good cases for inclusion, missed out.

As far as the money is concerned, this was new ground for us and I think it is fair to say that there was considerable consternation within and outside the game about the prospect of the England team gaining such riches overnight. It did not help that, in the time following the deal being done with Stanford and the England team departing for the Caribbean, the worldwide economic situation worsened and the country entered a state of recession. What were people to make of the cricket team earning a million dollars each in this way while so many supporters of the game were losing their jobs or struggling to make ends meet? We were all concerned about being made to look mercenary when we were representing our country. However, the bottom line was that the Stanford circus was about money. Perhaps our failure to recognize that fact led to our dismal performance and the confusion over what turned out to be a pretty sorry saga.

Of course, there was excitement within our ranks about the possibility of winning a million each, or a quarter of a million for those like me who were unlikely to play in the match, and in hindsight, I think we should have been much more open about how this trip could change our lives, more ruthless and cynical in our approach. We should have admitted we were playing for the money, and thought of ourselves as cricketing pirates in search of the loot. But if you are dragging the England name into something like this, you have a duty to respect that name and behave accordingly. We were not sure if we were allowed to express any excitement at all.

In the end, I think it was good for the image of the England team and the game that we didn't win that money, especially after what happened to Stanford in the months following the match. It turned out to be an unsettling week and much of that could be put down to the confusion about whether to be upfront and just say we were there solely for the money, or to treat the trip as the start of preparations for the tour to India.

Someone had bought the England team for a week and I for one felt uncomfortable about that. Was it really the national side who were out there? It was made all the more difficult by the antics of our American host. There could be no doubting that this was the Sir Allen Stanford Show, as was demonstrated when a particular bit of nonsense flared up in the middle of our week in Antigua. Stanford was clearly keen to get as much publicity from having the England team in his backyard as possible and, during one of the warm-up matches, that aim involved him becoming friendly with a group of our wives and girlfriends – including Alice. It was certainly bizarre to look up at the big screen and see Emily Prior, wife of wicketkeeper Matt, perched on the Texan's knee with Alice sitting to one side of him.

It was a difficult situation for the girls because the man who was strutting around as if he owned the place – which, to be fair, he did – decided to inflict himself upon them for a perfect photo opportunity. What were they supposed to do? Refuse to pose with him or be unfriendly? All they could do in the circumstances was grin and bear it.

I have to say that I wasn't particularly bothered. I could see it was all pretty harmless and was just Stanford being Stanford – in his mind, he had bought the rights to do exactly what he wanted – but I became bothered because Alice was bothered. It was strange seeing her picture in all the papers the next day and Alice didn't like it one little bit. She is just not into the WAG culture at all and she felt that she and Emily were being portrayed around the world as the epitome of modern WAGs. In truth, two more unlikely people than Alice and Emily to be caught up in something like that you could not wish to meet. It's just not them at all. So they got a bit upset about it and you couldn't really blame them. Stanford said afterwards he did not know it was the England partners he was flirting with and apologized, but I imagine he knew who they were and what he was doing.

The fuss blew over but the incident was symptomatic of the week, which culminated in our heavy defeat. The one good thing was to see the joy on the faces of some of the West Indies players, whose lives were changed by winning that money. Otherwise it was a good thing that the whole thing will not happen again.

However, I don't think what happened in Antigua had a detrimental effect on our spirit for the tour of India, which immediately followed. For me the journey was identical to the one I took from the Caribbean to India to make my Test debut almost three years earlier. I was looking forward to going back to the country where cricket is like a religion, and cricketers are treated like gods. I didn't play until the fifth and – as it turned out – final one-day international but couldn't help being caught up in the excitement generated by the tour.

We played in Rajkot and Cuttack, outposts where they had not seen too much of the national team, and the attitude towards both the home side and us was extraordinary. People congregated in their hundreds outside our hotel, waiting for a cricketer, any cricketer, to open a window so they could see him.

If a game started at 9 a.m., the ground would be full by 7 a.m., and the atmosphere was truly amazing every time we set foot on the park. The Indian side responded by playing fantastic 50-over cricket, which we struggled to live with, going 5–0 down in what was supposed to be a seven-match series before a highly distressing incident intervened.

I had finally made the team for that fifth match in Cuttack but had not scored very many as we lost again, and had settled down for a late-night bus ride back to our hotel in the nearby city of Bhubaneshwar. I slept on the bus and remember waking up as we got back to our base, and registering that I'd been sent some texts from home, saying something had happened in Mumbai. It turned out to be a terrorist attack on the Taj Mahal Hotel, our home away from home when we visited that great city.

At that stage, details were unclear and we were told not to panic and to get some sleep while our security man Reg Dickason found out what had happened. Some of us decided that sleep was not really an option and went to the hotel bar to try to find out what was going on from the TV. I remember Jimmy Anderson, Graeme Swann, Matt Prior and perhaps some others were there, and what we saw was very disturbing. It quickly became apparent that this was serious, and it was going on at our hotel – the place we loved to visit when we were in India, where our families always felt so comfortable and where we were due to return a week or so later. It is fair to say that it hit us hard emotionally.

The Taj Mahal Hotel is such a lovely place, one of the best hotels anyone could stay in. Now we were seeing graphic images of the most appalling scenes. The restaurant where we had eaten a couple of weeks earlier was being attacked and people we had met, and who had been so good to us, were being killed.

The attacks carried on through the night and I could not take my eyes off the TV. The Middlesex team were due to arrive at that very same hotel the next day for the Champions League and it all felt very close and very real, even though we were a long way from Mumbai.

What followed was a very long twenty-four hours. The players didn't really know what to do while the future of our tour was being discussed by the people in the know. A lot of players, myself included, wanted to get out of there as quickly as possible. It seemed a very volatile situation to us, and there had been reports that, in Mumbai, Westerners had been targeted by the terrorists. Should we be carrying on playing cricket in those circumstances?

Certainly, making that decision was very tough for Reg Dickason, captain Kevin Pietersen, coach Peter Moores, Hugh Morris, managing director of England cricket and John Carr of the ECB. Moving to Abu Dhabi was considered but, in the end, they decided that we should go home for a while while the situation was properly assessed, and I totally agreed with that. Eventually, we did go to the United Arab Emirates for a holding camp, after the last two one-day matches had been abandoned, while Reg compiled a report on whether it was safe for us to return to India for the scheduled two-match Test series.

Meanwhile, the mood in the camp was one of concern. Some players felt that if Reg, a highly respected figure, said it was safe to return, then we had to go, but others, including me, had reservations.

Our concerns were not totally down to security. We wondered whether it would be morally right to return to India to play cricket so soon after so many people had died in the awful attacks. Could cricket carry on in such circumstances? Shouldn't we postpone the matches now and return at some point in the future after a proper period had elapsed in which to mourn the dead? Those were the thoughts that were flashing through our minds.

When Reg arrived in Abu Dhabi, we had a meeting at our hotel. Reg began by standing up and saying that he was satisfied that a secure environment would be provided for us in India. That was enough for some players. It was left up to us to make our own choice. We were all in it together, but a few of us wanted more time to think about it and we went back to a room to discuss the situation. I couldn't help wondering whether the ECB were so keen to head back because India were such a rich and powerful cricketing nation but with hindsight I feel that was not the case. The ECB did not want to fall out with India and India wanted us to return but our welfare was very much part of the equation as far as the ECB were concerned too. In the end, we all felt we should go.

Now, looking back, I think I was right to ask questions and not to make a decision to return to India based on blind faith. I also think I was wrong to doubt Reg and the others in any way, because going back was definitely the right decision and I'm glad we went. It was a tough call but the decision was the correct one, although ultimately, we only knew for sure that we were doing the right thing when we saw what it meant to the people of India for us to be in Chennai for the first re-arranged Test. Only the peaceful nature of the rest of our tour proved Reg right, that and the reaction of the Indian people. They clearly wanted us to go back and we were extremely well-received throughout.

Maybe I was thinking too deeply about the politics of the situation because, once we were back, I certainly never felt ill at ease or in any way unsafe. That's how it had to be. Once we got back to India, we couldn't afford for anybody to be feeling they would rather be at home.

We played unbelievably well in that First Test in Chennai. It just showed that sometimes you don't need any preparation for a Test to perform at your best. It proves that cricket is very much a mental game.

However, we still lost on an emotional final day, which, I think, was just meant to be. For surely it was right that the great man of Mumbai himself, Sachin Tendulkar, should play the innings that won the match for India in record-breaking circumstances. We honestly felt that the game was out of our control towards the end. There was simply nothing we could do to stop Sachin winning the Test for his side. At that time, there was a TV advert running constantly in India in which a clearly emotional Sachin made a statesmanlike address, concluding, 'Now, more than ever, I play for India.' He sure did in that game.

The Second Test, in Mohali, was never likely to be as dramatic, not least because it was played in the north of India in winter, and the fog and cold played a part in a draw. But we again acquitted ourselves admirably, and if ever you could be satisfied with a Test series defeat, this was the occasion.

We returned home just in time for Christmas, and my birthday, and I felt that we had experienced enough in the way of incident to last us for the rest of the winter and longer. Surely we would have a smoother passage to the Caribbean? I thought wrong!

Barely a week after we arrived home came the bombshell that there was a serious problem between our captain and coach. I had no idea things were so bad between Pietersen and Moores. There had been no signs of real friction when we were in India. It was a quite extraordinary turn of events and a complete shock. People have subsequently asked me what went on but in those turbulent days of early January, I was reading the papers for information the same as everybody else.

The moment it all became public on New Year's Day, I felt that one of them would have to go because once it was out in the open it just seemed impossible that they could carry on working together. I just wondered how it had got to that stage, and I couldn't believe what I was hearing. I felt sorry for both of them but I thought it would be Moores who went, even though I couldn't see that he had done anything wrong. I was sure the ECB wouldn't sack Kevin – I just thought he would win that battle – and if the captain did not want the coach and had said so, the coach's position was untenable. When they both went, it surprised me, and I don't know how or why that decision was reached. I guess, with hindsight, it was the only thing the ECB could do in such a serious situation.

I did feel, however, that Moores was dealt a few harsh cards. He is a top man who only ever wanted what was best for the England team. He would bust a gut for the team. He cared almost too much. He couldn't relax or take his foot off the gas. Kev, meanwhile, was desperate to do well and was extremely ambitious both for himself and the team he was captaining. I am convinced he was doing what he thought was right, and it was so sad the situation ended in the way it did.

I don't think it was ever a personal thing between them. Kev just felt that Peter was not the right man to take England forward but once that opinion got into the public domain, it caused a terrible crisis, which was the last thing we needed at the start of an Ashes year.

The attempt to put it all behind us, and quickly, began under Andrew Strauss as captain and Andy Flower as coach, with me doing my bit as vice-captain on our tour of the West Indies, an appointment that I was honoured to accept.

As it turned out, the two Andys really steadied the ship. They are both strong men with a lot of fight and character and were just what were needed in such difficult circumstances. It was definitely the right decision to make Strauss the new captain ahead of me, and I was quite happy about that.

What I would say, too, is that Kevin was brilliant in settling back into the ranks. In many ways, he was made the scapegoat for what had happened but he put it all behind him as soon as we got to the Caribbean and he deserves immense credit for that.

We were certainly in the doldrums when we arrived in the Caribbean, and the situation was not helped by the debacle in the First Test in Jamaica when we were bowled out for 51. That was rock bottom – the only way from there was up.

A lot of straight talking was done in the aftermath of that First Test, and problems were raised openly and emotionally. Andy Flower, at that stage our interim coach, was in the chair. From that moment on we played a lot of good cricket and slowly but surely became credible Ashes challengers, even though we were not able to force a victory that would have given us a share of that Test series in the Caribbean.

I was, though, able to end a run of a year or so without a Test century and that was important to me. It was a massive relief, indeed, to get past seven Test centuries when I made number eight in Barbados, because it was an important step towards where I want to go and I had started to feel under pressure even though I was contributing half centuries.

I remain convinced that my problem was more mental than technical. I was so desperate to reach three figures again, I had started to beat myself up about it. Maybe I was trying too hard. It's that bar of soap thing – the more desperate you become to cling on to it, the more likely it is to squeeze out of your hand. I wasn't relaxed enough to make centuries during my run without one, and consequently I was making mistakes concentration-wise.

When another century followed in the Second Test against the West Indies in the return series at home, I was happy that I had overcome a personal obstacle. The fact that it was scored at Durham in partnership with Ravi Bopara, with whom I had played cricket since I was 14, made my ninth Test century one of my proudest moments – particularly as I walked off unbeaten at the end of the day's play with night-watchman Jimmy Anderson, my closest friend in the England team.

Our 2–0 victory over the West Indies not only allowed us to reclaim the Wisden Trophy just a few weeks after losing it, but it also got us back on the right path before the arrival of the Australians. Much was made of the poor quality of the West Indies but little was made of how well we played both at Lord's and Chester-le-Street.

The England team went on to contest the World Twenty20 tournament while I returned to Essex to make my first big, quick scores in Twenty20 cricket, an important development for me if I am to play in all forms of the game for England in the future. We all knew, though, that whatever happened in the first half of the 2009 summer was a warm-up for the main event. My first home Ashes series was upon me.

18

AN ASHES TRIUMPH!

I will never forget sitting in the home dressing room at The Oval with my team-mates after we had won the ultimate prize in Test cricket, the Ashes. All the support staff were there, and our families. There were kids running around, players talking, laughing and having a drink. Everyone was trying to take in the enormity of what we had just achieved, and what we had been through together, all the highs and lows of another dramatic series against the old enemy. Even now, as I write this a few days after the triumph, it is hard to take it all in.

When the big moment came on the fourth evening of the final Test, I am not sure any of us really knew what to do. Look at the pictures. After Graeme Swann took the wicket of century-maker Mike Hussey, the final one to fall, England players are running everywhere, in all directions, shouting and screaming wildly. Look again and you'll see me slipping the ball in my pocket. I took the catch to clinch the Ashes at short leg, although I was hardly expecting it because Hussey had not looked as if he would provide a chance all day.

I remembered a question and answer session at my old school, Bedford, when coach Derek Randall had told of how he had taken a catch to win a series for England and had always regretted not keeping hold of the ball. I was not going to let this one out of my clutches at any point. As I ran around not knowing what to do with myself, all I could think was, 'Don't lose the ball!' It's my souvenir of the biggest day in my cricketing career so far, and I will be putting it on display at home as a constant reminder of the day I helped England win the Ashes.

So how did we reach the stage where our biggest cricketing dream had come true and we were Ashes winners for the second successive home series? Many people felt we had no hope of achieving that goal when we were thrashed in the Fourth Test at Headingley to relinquish our 1–0 series lead.

We succeeded because we seized the crucial moments in the series, retained our belief when people doubted us and produced a genuine team effort that, in the end, proved too much for Australia. The 2005 series was a classic, when England won the Ashes for the first time in nearly 20 attempts, but the 2009 was not far behind in terms of sporting drama and twists and turns. And, gloriously for England, it had the same happy outcome.

The countdown had seemed endless and when the big day – Wednesday, 8 July – finally arrived, it is fair to say that we were not at our absolute best. Maybe it was nerves. Maybe it was the fact that, in Cardiff's Swalec Stadium, we were taking a step into the unknown – the venue had never before staged a five-day game, let alone such a big match. Whatever the reason may have been, we just did not seem to handle the week of the First Test particularly well as a team, although the people of Wales did England proud over those historic five days. Glamorgan put on a fantastic show, the crowd gave us tremendous support and the stadium was absolutely worthy of the magnitude of the event.

We started off pretty well after winning the toss and electing to bat. Virtually all of us got starts, and even though I was disappointed to get out for 10 we felt we had made a reasonable score in 435 all out. Okay, maybe there was some poor shot selection at times but we felt that the score gave us a chance of dictating the state of the game.

We were quickly put right on that one. We'd gone in to the match with a two-spinner attack in Graeme Swann and Monty Panesar, and Australia replied with the small matter of 674 for six declared, four of their batsmen scoring centuries. We always knew that Australia would provide the toughest of opponents – they were, after all, the number one ranked side in the world – but if ever we needed to be reminded of the extent of the task ahead of us, then this was the occasion.

We were up against it after that, but our first lucky break came on the fourth day when we were struggling to stay in the game and rain washed out play after tea. It enabled us to regroup ahead of the final day, a Sunday, but we were still very much on the back foot, particularly when we were five wickets down at lunch with only a draw to play for. I must confess that there was not too much optimism in our dressing room at that stage. As a cricketer you never give up on a bad situation until the last wicket falls, but I couldn't really see any way out of this one.

Thankfully, though, we had Paul Collingwood in our team,

a batsman who has consistently prospered when the chips are down both for himself and his team. Colly managed to frustrate Australia, firstly in partnership with Andrew Flintoff and then with our lower order, until he was out for 74 with 11.3 overs remaining and just Jimmy Anderson and Monty left at the wicket.

No hope? We thought so, but incredibly the two coolest and most confident people on the ground were Jimmy and Monty. When everyone else had given up on them, including myself and Colly, who were their designated batting 'buddies', they remained focused on the job in hand, blocking out all distractions.

There was a bit of fuss over us sending on our physio to try to slow the game down in the last few overs and enable them to stay on top of the situation, but clearly Jimmy and Monty did not need any distractions or slowing up of proceedings. I can honestly say they were never in danger and they managed to get through to the close without any alarms.

So, amazingly, the First Test was drawn, against all the odds, and we were able to regroup before we made our way to a venue where we felt much more at home, Lord's, for the Second Test. We had talked about needing to show fighting spirit after we were bowled out for 51 in Jamaica, and ultimately, that bit of tail-end resistance, when two of our number had knuckled down to a dog-fight, or whatever you want to call it, was going to have a huge impact on our chances of winning the Ashes.

Lord's is a fantastic place to play any cricket, let alone an Ashes Test. England may not have beaten Australia there for

75 years but that did not make us feel any the less comfortable, particularly after the great escape in Cardiff. As one of our number said before the Second Test, 'This is more like it. We're back where we belong now, at Lord's. We'll be much better here.' And we were. On a personal note, Lord's was where I made my biggest individual contribution to the series.

Before the match, Andrew Flintoff announced that he would retire from Test cricket at the end of the series, and then, on the last day, produced a great spell of sustained, hostile fast bowling that put us 1–0 up.

Freddie had told a few of us what he intended to do, ahead of his announcement, and I could fully understand his reasoning. There had been speculation about whether it might be his last series and he decided it was best to get his situation out in the open so that everyone knew where he stood.

It is such a shame that the injuries Freddie has had to endure for so long had finally become too much for him to play Test cricket any more. His body was basically saying to him 'no more' and we all had sympathy for Flintoff as well as huge admiration for what he has achieved in the game.

I was surprised that some people thought he was being selfish in making his plans public, or that his decision might in some way be a distraction during the Ashes series. I could not see why it should be. Better surely to know where you stand rather than having people saying 'will he or won't he' throughout the series.

It certainly did not have an adverse affect on us at the start of the Second Test because, after again winning the toss,

Andrew Strauss and I put on 196 for the first wicket in very good time and England had made the most positive of starts.

For me 96 was a satisfying score but I was very annoyed with myself that I could not turn it into three figures. Those extra four runs really do make all the difference to any batsman. It was particularly frustrating for me that I did not go on to more when we subsequently fell short of where we should have been after such a good start, slipping to 425 all out with Ben Hilfenhaus, something of a surprise choice in the Australian attack at the start of the series, again impressing with his swing bowling.

But any worries that we may have underachieved were quickly put to the back of our minds when Anderson and Graham Onions, making his first Ashes appearance, were the key performers in bowling Australia out for 215.

There was some talk about whether we should have enforced the follow-on but I never had any doubts that it was the right thing not to, and when we again batted well in our second innings, we were in with a fantastic opportunity of winning the Test and making our own little bit of Lord's history.

We had a nervous time on the fourth evening when it looked as though, on a good pitch, Australia still had a chance of making history themselves by chasing the biggest target ever reached to win a Test. That they did not succeed was almost totally down to Flintoff. What a magnificent spell he produced – eleven of the best overs I have ever seen in a Test match. All bar one delivery, I believe, were delivered at a speed in excess of 90 miles per hour, and the Australians just could not cope. Freddie was unhittable. Considering he was struggling with a knee injury that was serious enough to necessitate his imminent retirement, it really was an extraordinary performance. Australia were 406 all out and we were triumphant by 115 runs. One up, three to play!

We had the better of the Third Test at Edgbaston but the game was badly affected by the weather. Even so, we had a chance to win it on the last day but, again, Australia showed that they were not number one for nothing, and batted with intent, determination and no little skill to keep us at bay.

We had had to go into the match without Pietersen, whose Achilles injury was clearly restricting him throughout the Lord's Test. Kevin was given the awful news that his series was over because he needed an operation, a huge blow for him and a complete contrast with the 2005 series when he emerged as the last-day Ashes winner. We all felt for him and knew we had to redouble our efforts without him.

It was disappointing that we did not make more inroads into the Australian batting on that final day but it should be remembered that the Edgbaston pitch was, in effect, a third-day pitch because of the weather, so it was never going to be an easy task. We were still in very good spirits at the end of the match, happy that we were ahead with just two games to go. Excitement was building along with the feeling that we might be on the verge of something special, which is why Headingley was such a massive disappointment. It really was an awful Test for us. We were beaten so badly that a lesser side could have been irreparably damaged.

It started with Flintoff being ruled out on fitness grounds, the management deciding that back to back Tests were just too much for his knee. Then, on the first morning of the match, we were plunged into more uncertainty when Matt Prior experienced a back spasm during our warm-ups and, for a while, looked as though he would be ruled out of the match.

Eventually Matt was okay to play but the tone appeared to have been set for a completely miserable three days. We were totally outplayed and lost our precious advantage in the series. It is hard to put my finger on why it happened but the bottom line is that we were awful and Australia were brilliant.

Once again, this was where Andy Flower came into his own. Our team director had chaired a very open team meeting when we had crashed to defeat in Jamaica at the start of our West Indian tour early in 2009, and now he summoned us straight after the match for another no-holds-barred exchange of views. Andy is not afraid to ruffle feathers but he has everyone's respect and he is a brilliant man-manager and coach. Things were said that had better remain private but by the time we left Leeds we had already put the Fourth Test debacle behind us and were ready for the finale to the series, a winner takes all Test to win the Ashes.

It took me back a bit to see everyone writing us off. We had gone from heroes to zero very quickly, it seemed to me, and before the series had even ended. But the important thing was that we believed we could do it and we were determined to prove it at The Oval, scene of the draw in 2005 that sparked off scenes of such wild celebration when Michael Vaughan's team won the Ashes.

Strauss won another important toss – one of those breaks that went our way throughout the summer – and we put 332 on the board on what was turning out to be a very dry pitch. It was starting to crumble on the first day. Again, there were those who thought we might have underachieved in not getting 400 but we knew it could only get harder to bat as the match went on. What we did not know was that Stuart Broad was about to produce another great spell of fast bowling.

In all, eight Australian wickets fell in one session on the second day of the final Test, five of them to Broad, an extra-ordinary turn of events that helped seal the destination of the Ashes – as, too, did a century on debut from Jonathan Trott. Jonathan had come in for Ravi Bopara and showed great character and temperament to reach three figures in the second innings of his first match at the highest level.

It left Australia with the small matter of having to score 546 to win the match and the Ashes, a target that had never been successfully chased in any first-class match before, let alone a Test match.

It could not be done, could it? No, as it turned out, it could not, but Australia battled all the way and made life hard for us, as you would expect, on that historic Sunday in South London. However, despite some nervous moments, I can honestly say I never had any doubts that we would win the game, unlike at Lord's when I was worried going into the last day. And when Flintoff ran out Ricky Ponting from mid on, we knew it just had to be our day and our year.

Of course, I was delighted to have been part of the moment when the urn was won. No, it had not been the greatest of series for me with the bat, but that could not take any of the gloss off the achievement as far as I was concerned.

STARTING OUT – MY STORY SO FAR

We had a lovely time with our families and I had a good chat with Mike Hussey, who had held us up on that last day. He has had a bit of a lean spell and he told me to remember how I had got to the England team and scored hundreds in the first place. He said that I was not doing too much wrong and it was important to keep my lack of big runs in the series in perspective. I don't think I have to change my game drastically, or panic that the runs have dried up. My methods and technique have been good enough to get me the record I have achieved in my three years in the England team and I am confident that, with hard work, there will be plenty more runs again in the future.

Back at our hotel near Tower Bridge the party went on long into the night – not with the excesses of 2005, perhaps, but none the less special for that. Those who had won the Ashes before talked of trying to savour it a bit more this time, making sure the moment did not pass them by. In 2005 England had not won the Ashes for so long, but this time there was a sense that this was just the beginning.

We are still, at the time of writing, the fifth best Test team in the world but we are Ashes winners and that is something I will cherish forever. I also know that there is a long and exciting journey ahead for us if we are to progress to being the best team in the world. Andrew Strauss and Andy Flower have been the key figures in getting us to this stage and they will be integral to us achieving our goal. I very much want to be part of that journey. The good times, I hope, have only just begun.

ALASTAIR COOK IN TEST CRICKET

COMPILED BY VICTOR ISAACS

Test Career Record (2005/2006–2008) – *up to and including Fourth Test v South Africa at The Oval*

M	I	NO	Runs	HS	Avge	S/R	100s	50s
34	62	2	2573	127	42.88	46.29	7	14

1. v India at Nagpur 1–3 March 2006 – Match drawn

Toss: England
England 393 (P.D.Collingwood 134*) & 297–3dec (A.N.Cook 104*); India 323 (M.J.Hoggard 6–57) & 260–6 (W.Jaffer 100)

1st innings	b I.K.Pathan	60
2nd innings	not out	104

Match highlights:
Test match debut aged 21 years and 66 days – the 26th youngest England debutant. Cook was the fifth English player to score a half-century and a century on his debut.

2. v India at Mohali 9–13 March 2006 – India won by 9 wickets

Toss: England
England 300 (A.Kumble 5–76) & 181; India 338 & 144–1

1st innings	lbw b I.K.Pathan	17
2nd innings	c M.S.Dhoni b M.M.Patel	2

3. v Sri Lanka at Lord's 11–15 May 2006 – Match drawn

Toss: England

STARTING OUT - MY STORY SO FAR

England 551–6dec (M.E.Trescothick 106, K.P.Pietersen 158); Sri Lanka 192 &
537–9
(D.P.M.D.Jayawardene 119)

1st innings   c K.C.Sangakkara b M.F.Maharoof   89

4. v Sri Lanka at Birmingham 25–28 May 2006 – England won by 6 wickets

Toss: Sri Lanka
Sri Lanka 141 & 231 (M.G.Vandort 105); England 295 (K.P.Pietersen 142,
M.Muralitharan 6–86) & 81–4

1st innings   lbw b M.Muralitharan   23
2nd innings   not out   34

5. v Sri Lanka at Nottingham – 2–5 June 2006 – Sri Lanka won by 134 runs

Toss: Sri Lanka
Sri Lanka 231 & 322 (M.S.Panesar 5–78); England 229 & 190 (M.Muralitharan 8–70)

1st innings   b S.L.Malinga   24
2nd innings   lbw b M.Muralitharan   5

6. v Pakistan at Lord's 13–17 July 2006 – Match drawn

Toss: England
England 528–9dec (A.N.Cook 105, P.D.Collingwood 186, I.R.Bell 100*) & 296–
8dec (A.J.Strauss 128); Pakistan 445 (Mohammad Yousuf 202) & 214–4

1st innings   b Mohammad Sami   105
2nd innings   c Mohammad Yousuf b Umar Gul   4

Match highlights:
*He became the second youngest English batsman, after D.C.S. Compton, to record
a century at Lord's (aged 21 years and 200 days).*

7. v Pakistan at Manchester 27–29 July 2006 – England won by an innings and 120 runs

Toss: Pakistan
Pakistan 119 (S.J.Harmison 6–19) & 222 (S.J.Harmison 5–57, M.S.Panesar 5–72);
England 461–9dec (A.N.Cook 127, I.R.Bell 106*)
1st innings   lbw b Umar Gul   127

8. **v Pakistan at Leeds 4–8 August 2006 – England won by 167 runs**
Toss: England
England 515 (K.P.Pietersen 135, I.R.Bell 119, Umar Gul 5–123) & 345 (A.J.Strauss 116); Pakistan 538 (Younis Khan 173, Mohammad Yousuf 192) & 155

1st innings	c and b Umar Gul	23
2nd innings	c Faisal Iqbal b Danish Kaneria	21

9. **v Pakistan at The Oval 17–21 August 2006 – Match drawn**
Toss: Pakistan
England 173 & 298–4; Pakistan 504 (Mohammad Yousuf 128)

1st innings	lbw b Shahid Nazir	40
2nd innings	lbw b Umar Gul	83

Match highlights:
This match ended at tea on the fourth day when Pakistan refused to take the field. The result was originally recorded as a concession victory to England but has now been changed to match drawn.

10. **v Australia at Brisbane 23–27 November 2006 – Australia won by 277 runs**
Toss: Australia
Australia 602–9dec (R.T.Ponting 196) & 202–1dec (J.L.Langer 100*); England 157 (G.D.McGrath 6–50) & 370

1st innings	c S.K.Warne b G.D.McGrath 11
2nd innings	c M.E.K.Hussey b S.K.Warne 43

11. **v Australia at Adelaide 1–5 December 2006 – Australia won by 6 wickets**
Toss: England
England 551–6dec (P.D.Collingwood 206, K.P.Pietersen 158) & 129; Australia 513 (R.T.Ponting 142, M.J.Clarke 124, M.J.Hoggard 7–109) & 168–4

1st innings	c A.C.Gilchrist b S.R.Clark	27
2nd innings	c A.C.Gilchrist b S.R.Clark	9

12. **v Australia at Perth 14–18 December 2006 – Australia won by 206 runs**
Toss: Australia
Australia 244 (M.S.Panesar 5–92) & 527–5dec (M.E.K.Hussey 103, M.J.Clarke 135*, A.C.Gilchrist 102*); England 215 & 350 (A.N.Cook 116)

| 1st innings | c J.L.Langer b G.D.McGrath | 15 |
| 2nd innings | c A.C.Gilchrist b G.D.McGrath | 116 |

Match highlights:
Cook hit his fourth Test match century and also became the 10th Test match batsman to record four Test centuries or more before they turned 22 years of age.

13. v Australia at Melbourne 26–28 December 2006 – Australia won by an innings and 99 runs

Toss: England
England 159 (S.K.Warne 5–39) & 161; Australia 419 (M.L.Hayden 153, A.Symonds 156)

| 1st innings | c A.C.Gilchrist b B.Lee | 11 |
| 2nd innings | b S.R.Clark | 20 |

Match highlights:
Cook passed 1,000 Test match runs during the second innings of this match. S.K. Warne took his 700th Test match wicket when he dismissed A.J. Strauss in England's first innings.

14. v Australia at Sydney 2–5 January 2007 – Australia won by 10 wickets

Toss: England
England 291 & 147; Australia 393 & 46–0

| 1st innings | c A.C.Gilchrist b S.R.Clark | 20 |
| 2nd innings | c A.C.Gilchrist b B.Lee | 4 |

Match highlights:
England lost the Ashes by five games to nil – only the second time in Ashes history this result has been recorded.

15. v West Indies at Lord's 17–21 May 2007 – Match drawn

Toss: West Indies
England 553–5dec (A.N.Cook 105, P.D.Collingwood 111, I.R.Bell 109*, M.J.Prior 126*) & 284–8dec (K.P.Pietersen 109); West Indies 437 (M.S.Panesar 6–129) & 89–0

| 1st innings | c D.J.Bravo b J.E.Taylor | 105 |
| 2nd innings | c D.Ramdin b C.D.Collymore | 65 |

16. v West Indies at Leeds 25–28 May 2007 – England won by an innings and 283 runs
Toss: England
England 570–7dec (M.P.Vaughan 103, K.P.Pietersen 226); West Indies 146 & 141

1st innings   lbw b C.H.Gayle   42

17. v West Indies at Manchester 7–11 June 2007 – England won by 60 runs
Toss: England
England 370 & 313 (A.N.Cook 106, D.J.G.Sammy 7–66); West Indies 229 & 394 (S.Chanderpaul 116*, M.S.Panesar 6–137)

1st innings   c D.J.Bravo b D.J.G.Sammy   60
2nd innings   lbw b C.H.Gayle   106

Match highlights:
Cook recorded his sixth Test match century (aged 22 years and 164 days). Only D.G. Bradman, G.A. Headley, G.S. Sobers, Javed Miandad, R.N. Harvey and S.R. Tendulkar have recorded six or more centuries by the same age.

18. v West Indies at Chester-le-Street 15–18 June 2007 – England won by 7 wickets
Toss: England
West Indies 287 (S.Chanderpaul 136*, R.J.Sidebottom 5–88) & 222 (M.S. Panesar 5–46); England 400 (P.D.Collingwood 128, F.H.Edwards 5–112) & 111–3

1st innings   c D.Ramdin b F.H.Edwards   13
2nd innings   c D.J.Bravo b D.B-L.Powell   7

19. v India at Lord's 19–23 July 2007 – Match drawn
Toss: England
England 298 & 282 (K.P.Pietersen 134, R.P.Singh 5–59); India 201 (J.M. Anderson 5–42) & 282–9

1st innings   lbw b S.C.Ganguly 36
2nd innings   lbw b Z.Khan   17

20. v India at Nottingham 27–31 July 2007 – India won by 7 wickets
Toss: India
England 198 & 355 (M.P.Vaughan 124, Z.Khan 5–75); India 481 & 73–3

1st innings   lbw b S.C.Ganguly 43
2nd innings   lbw b Z.Khan   23

Match highlights:
Cook passed 1,500 Test match runs during his first innings.

21. v India at The Oval 9–13 August 2007 – Match drawn

Toss: India
India 664 (A.Kumble 110*) & 180–6dec; England 345 & 369–6 (K.P.Pietersen 101)
1st innings   c R.P.Singh b A.Kumble   61
2nd innings   c V.V.S.Laxman b A.Kumble 43

22. v Sri Lanka at Kandy 1–5 December 2007 – Sri Lanka won by 88 runs

Toss: Sri Lanka
Sri Lanka 188 & 442–8dec (K.C.Sangakkara 152); England 281 (M.Muralitharan 6–55) & 261

1st innings   lbw b W.P.U.J.C.Vaas   0
2nd innings   c L.P.C.Silva b W.P.U.J.C.Vaas   4

Match highlights:
During England's first innings, M. Muralitharan claimed the world record for wickets taken when he dismissed P.D. Collingwood.

23. v Sri Lanka at Colombo (SSC) 9–13 December 2007 – Match drawn

Toss: England
England 351 (M.Muralitharan 5–116) & 250–3; Sri Lanka 548–9dec (M.G.Vandort 138, D.P.M.D.Jayawardene 195)

1st innings   lbw b S.L.Malinga   81
2nd innings   c D.P.M.D.Jayawardene b L.P.C.Silva 62

24. v Sri Lanka at Galle 18–22 December 2007 – Match drawn

Toss: England
Sri Lanka 499–8dec (D.P.M.D.Jayawardene 213*); England 81 & 251–6 (A.N.Cook 118)

1st innings   c H.A.P.W.Jayawardene b W.P.U.J.C.Vaas   13
2nd innings   c H.A.P.W.Jayawardene b U.W.M.B.C.A.Welegedara   118

Match highlights:
Cook became the first Englishman to record seven centuries before his twenty-third birthday.

25. v New Zealand at Hamilton 5–9 March 2008 – New Zealand won by 189 runs
Toss: New Zealand
New Zealand 470 (L.R.P.L.Taylor 120) & 177–9dec (R.J.Sidebottom 6–49);
England 348 & 110
1st innings   c sub (NKW Horsley) b C.S.Martin   38
2nd innings   c B.B.McCullum b K.D.Mills   13

26. v New Zealand at Wellington 13–17 March 2008 – England won by 126 runs
Toss: New Zealand
England 342 (T.R.Ambrose 102) & 293; New Zealand 198 (J.M.Anderson 5–73)
& 311 (R.J.Sidebottom 5–105)

1st innings   c B.B.McCullum b J.D.P.Oram   44
2nd innings   c S.P.Fleming b K.D.Mills   60

Match highlights:
Cook passed 2,000 Test match runs during the second innings of this match.

27. v New Zealand at Napier 22–26 March 2008 – England won by 121 runs
Toss: England
England 253 (K.P.Pietersen 129, T.G.Southee 5–55) & 467–7dec (A.J.Strauss 177,
I.R.Bell 110); New Zealand 168 (R.J.Sidebottom 7–47) & 431 (M.S.Panesar 6–126)

1st innings   b C.S.Martin   2
2nd innings   c B.B.McCullum b J.S.Patel   37

28. v New Zealand at Lord's 15–19 May 2008 – Match drawn
Toss: England
New Zealand 277 & 269–6 (J.D.P.Oram 101); England 319 (M.P.Vaughan 106,
D.L.Vettori 5–69)

1st innings   c B.B.McCullum b C.S.Martin   61

29. v New Zealand at Manchester 23–26 May 2008 – England won by 6 wickets
Toss: New Zealand
New Zealand 381 (L.R.P.L.Taylor 154*) & 114 (M.S.Panesar 6–37); England 202
(D.L.Vettori 5–66) & 294–4 (A.J.Strauss 106)

| 1st innings | lbw b I.E.O'Brien | 19 |
| 2nd innings | c J.A.H.Marshall b D.L.Vettori | 28 |

30. v New Zealand at Nottingham 5–8 June 2008 – England won by an innings and 9 runs
Toss: New Zealand
England 364 (K.P.Pietersen 115); New Zealand 123 (J.M.Anderson 7–43) & 232 (R.J.Sidebottom 6–67)

| 1st innings | b K.D.Mills | 6 |

30. v New Zealand at Nottingham 5–8 June 2008 – England won by an innings and 9 runs
Toss: New Zealand
England 364 (K.P.Pietersen 115); New Zealand 123 (J.M.Anderson 7–43) & 232 (R.J.Sidebottom 6–67)

| 1st innings | b K.D.Mills | 6 |

31. v South Africa at Lord's 10–14 July 2008 – Match drawn
Toss: South Africa
England 593–8dec (I.R.Bell 199, K.P.Pietersen 152); South Africa 247 (A.G.Prince 101) & 393–3dec (N.D.McKenzie 138, G.C.Smith 107, H.M.Amla 104*)

| 1st innings | c A.B.de Villiers b M.Morkel | 60 |

32. v South Africa at Leeds 18–21 July 2008 – South Africa won by 10 wickets
Toss: South Africa
England 203 & 327; South Africa 522 (A.B.de Villiers 174, A.G.Prince 149) & 9–0

| 1st innings | c M.V.Boucher b M.Morkel | 18 |
| 2nd innings | c H.M.Amla b J.H.Kallis | 60 |

33. v South Africa at Birmingham 30 July–2 August 2008 – South Africa won by 5 wickets
Toss: England
England 231 & 363 (P.D.Collingwood 135); South Africa 314 & 283–5 (G.C.Smith 154*)

| 1st innings | c J.H.Kallis b A.Nel | 76 |
| 2nd innings | c M.V.Boucher b M.Ntini | 9 |

34. v South Africa at The Oval 7–11 August 2008 – England won by 6 wickets
Toss: South Africa
South Africa 194 & 318; England 316 (K.P.Pietersen 100, M.Ntini 5–94) & 198–4

| 1st innings | c M.V.Boucher b M.Ntini | 39 |
| 2nd innings | c G.C.Smith b M.Ntini | 67 |

Match highlights:
Cook passed 2,500 Test match runs during the second innings of this match.

35. v India at Chennai 11–15 December 2008 – India won by 6 wickets
Toss: England
England 316 (A.J.Strauss 123) & 311–9dec (A.J.Strauss 108, P.D.Collingwood 108); India 241 & 387–4 S.R.Tendulkar 103*)

| 1st innings | c Z.Khan b Harbhajan Singh 52 |
| 2nd innings | c M.S.Dhoni b I.Sharma | 9 |

36. v India at Mohali 19–23 December 2008 – Match drawn
Toss: India
India 453 (G.Gambhir 179, R.S.Dravid 136) & 251–7dec; England 302 (K.P.Pietersen 144) & 64–1

| 1st innings | lbw b Z.Khan | 50 |
| 2nd innings | c V.V.S.Laxman b I.Sharma | 10 |

37. v West Indies at Kingston 4–7 February 2009 – West Indies won by an innings and 23 runs
Toss: England
England 318 & 51 (J.E.Taylor 5–11); West Indies 392 (C.H.Gayle 104, R.R.Sarwan 107, S.C.J.Broad 5–85)

| 1st innings | c R.R.Sarwan b D.B-L.Powell 4 |
| 2nd innings | c D.S.Smith b J.E.Taylor | 0 |

38. v West Indies at North Sound 13 February 2009 – Match drawn
Toss: West Indies
England 7–0; West Indies did not bat

| 1st innings | not out 1 |

Match highlights:
Match was abandoned after just 10 balls due to the dangerously sandy outfield.

39. v West Indies at St Johns 15–19 February 2009 – Match drawn
Toss: West Indies
England 566–9dec (A.J.Strauss 169, P.D.Collingwood 113) & 221–8dec; West
Indies 285 (G.P.Swann 5–57) & 370–9 (R.R.Sarwan 106)

1st innings	c D.S.Smith b C.H.Gayle	52
2nd innings	c D.S.Smith b R.O.Hinds	58

40. v West Indies at Bridgetown 26 February–2 March 2009 – Match drawn
Toss: England
England 600–6dec (A.J.Strauss 142, R.S.Bopara 104) & 279–2dec (A.N.Cook
139*); West Indies 749–9dec (R.R.Sarwan 291, D.Ramdin 166, G.P.Swann 5–165)

1st innings	c R.O.Hinds b J.E.Taylor	94
2nd innings	not out	139

Match highlights:
*Cook passed 3,000 Test match runs when he reached 97 in the second innings; and
passed his previous career Test best in the second innings while recording his eighth
Test century and his first since December 2007 at Galle in Sri Lanka.*

41. v West Indies at Port of Spain 6–10 March 2009 – Match drawn
Toss: England
England 546–6dec (A.J.Strauss 142, P.D.Collingwood 161, M.J.Prior 131*) &
237–6dec (K.P.Pietersen 102); West Indies 544 (C.H.Gayle 102, S.Chanderpaul
147*, B.P.Nash 109) & 114–8

1st innings	c D.Ramdin b D.B-L.Powell	12
2nd innings	c D.Ramdin b R.O.Hinds	24

42. v West Indies at Lord's 6–8 May 2009 – England won by 10 wickets
Toss: West Indies
England 377 (R.S.Bopara 143, F.H.Edwards 6–92) & 32–0; West Indies 152
(G.Onions 5–38) & 256

1st innings	b F.H.Edwards	35
2nd innings	not out	14

43. v West Indies at Chester-le-Street 14–18 May 2009 – won by an innings and 83 runs

Toss: England
England 569–6dec (A.N.Cook 160, R.S.Bopara 108); West Indies 310
(R.R.Sarwan 100, J.M.Anderson 5–87) & 176

1st innings	c C.H.Gayle b S.J.Benn	160

Match highlights:
Cook recorded his ninth Test match century while also passing his previous career Test best.

44. v Australia at Cardiff 8–12 July 2009 – Match drawn

Toss: England
England 435 & 252; Australia 674–6dec (S.M.Katich 122, R.T.Ponting 150,
M.J.North 125*, B.J.Haddin 121)

1st innings	c M.E.K.Hussey b B.W.Hilfenhaus	10
2nd innings	lbw b M.G.Johnson	6

45. v Australia at Lord's 16–20 July 2009 – England won by 115 runs

Toss: England
England 425 (A.J.Strauss 161) & 311–6dec; Australia 215 & 406 (M.J.Clarke 136,
A.Flintoff 5–92)

1st innings	lbw b M.G.Johnson	95
2nd innings	lbw b N.M.Hauritz	32

46. v Australia at Edgbaston 30 July-3 August 2009 – Match drawn

Toss: Australia
Australia 263 (J.M.Anderson 5–80) & 375–5 (M.J.Clarke 103*); England 376

1st innings	c G.A.Manou b P.M.Siddle	o

47. v Australia at Headingley 7–9 August 2009 – Australia won by an innings and 80 runs

Toss: England
England 102 (P.M.Siddle 5–21) & 263 (M.G.Johnson 5–69); Australia 445
(M.J.North 110, S.C.J.Broad 6–91)

1st innings	c M.J.Clarke b S.R.Clark	30
2nd innings	c B.J.Haddin b M.G.Johnson	30

48. v Australia at The Oval 20–23 August 2009 – won by 197 runs

Toss: England

England 332 & 373–9dec (I.J.L.Trott 119); Australia 160 (S.C.J.Broad 5–37) & 348 (M.E.K.Hussey 121)

1st innings	c R.T.Ponting b P.M.Siddle	10
2nd innings	c M.J.Clarke b M.J.North	9

Notes:

Passed 3,500 Test runs when he reached 10 in the first innings

ALASTAIR COOK IN ONE-DAY INTERNATIONAL CRICKET

COMPILED BY VICTOR ISAACS

One-Day International Career Record (2006–2008) – *up to and including New Zealand at Lord's 28 June 2008*

M	I	NO	Runs	HS	Avge	S/R	100s	50s
22	22	0	691	102	31.40	68.08	1	3

1. v Sri Lanka at Manchester 28 June 2006 – Sri Lanka won by 33 runs
Toss: Sri Lanka
Sri Lanka 318–7 (50 overs) (W.U.Tharanga 60, D.P.M.D.Jayawardene 100, M.F.Maharoof 58*); England 285 (48.4 overs)

b C.R.D.Fernando   39   (38 balls; 8 fours)

Match highlights:
One-day international debut aged 21 years and 17 days – the 11th youngest England debutant.

2. v Sri Lanka at Leeds 1 July 2006 – Sri Lanka won by 8 wickets
Toss: England
England 321–7 (50 overs) (M.E.Trescothick 121, S.L.Malinga 4–44); Sri Lanka 324–2 (37.3 overs)
(W.U.Tharanga 109, S.T.Jayasuriya 152)

c D.P.M.D.Jayawardene b M.F.Maharoof   41   (54 balls; 4 fours)

3. v West Indies at Lord's 1 July 2007 – England won by 79 runs
Toss: West Indies
England 225 (49.5 overs) (I.R.Bell 56, F.H.Edwards 5–45); West Indies 146 (39.5 overs) (S.Chanderpaul 53)

c D.J.Bravo b F.H.Edwards   29   (47 balls; 3 fours)

4. v West Indies at Birmingham 4 July 2007 – West Indies won by 61 runs
Toss: England
West Indies 278–5 (50 overs) (S.Chanderpaul 116*, M.N.Samuels 77); England 217 (46 overs) (M.J.Prior 52, R.Rampaul 4–41)

c F.H.Edwards b D.B-L.Powell   19   (24 balls; 3 fours)

5. v West Indies at Nottingham 7 July 2007 – West Indies won by 93 runs
Toss: West Indies
West Indies 289–5 (50 overs) (C.H.Gayle 82, R.S.Morton 82*); England 196 (44.2 overs) (O.A.Shah 51, D.B-L.Powell 4–40)

c D.R.Smith b D.B-L.Powell   18   (27 balls; 4 fours)

6. v India at Southampton 21 August 2007 – England won by 104 runs
Toss: India
England 288–2 (50 overs) (A.N.Cook 102, I.R.Bell 126*); India 184 (50 overs) (J.M.Anderson 4–23)

b R.P.Singh   102   (126 balls; 8 fours)

Match highlights:
Cook recorded his first and only one-day international century.

7. v India at Bristol 24 August 2007 – India won by 9 runs
Toss: India
India 329–7 (50 overs) (S.R.Tendulkar 99, R.S.Dravid 92, A.Flintoff 5–56); England 320–8 (50 overs) (I.R.Bell 64, A.D.Mascarenhas 52)

c M.S.Dhoni b M.M.Patel   36   (41 balls; 8 fours)

8. v India at Birmingham 27 August 2007 – England won by 42 runs
Toss: India
England 281–8 (50 overs) (I.R.Bell 79); India 239 (48.1 overs) (S.C.Ganguly 72, R.S.Dravid 56)

c Yuvraj Singh b R.R.Powar   40   (56 balls, 4 fours)

9. v India at Manchester 30 August 2007 – England won by 3 wickets
Toss: India
India 212 (49.4 overs) (S.R.Tendulkar 55, Yuvraj Singh 71, S.C.J.Broad 4–51);
England 213–7 (48 overs) (A.B.Agarkar 4–60)

b Z.Khan   0   (2 balls)

10. v India at Leeds 2 September 2007 – India won by 38 runs (D/L)
Toss: England
India 324–6 (50 overs) (S.C.Ganguly 59, S.R.Tendulkar 71, G.Gambhir 51, Yuvraj
Singh 72); England 242–8 (39 overs) (P.D.Collingwood 91*)

c M.S.Dhoni b A.B.Agarkar   4   (11 balls)

11. v India at The Oval 5 September 2007 – India won by 2 wickets
Toss: England
England 316–6 (50 overs) (K.P.Pietersen 53, O.A.Shah 107*, L.J.Wright 50);
India 317–8 (49.4 overs) (S.C.Ganguly 53, S.R.Tendulkar 94)

c M.S.Dhoni b Z.Khan   0   (2 balls)

12. v Sri Lanka at Dambulla 1 October 2007 – Sri Lanka won by 119 runs
Toss: Sri Lanka
Sri Lanka 269–7 (50 overs) (D.P.M.D.Jayawardene 66); England 150 (34.5 overs)
(M.F.Maharoof 4–31)

c K.C.Sangakkara b M.F.Maharoof   46   (80 balls; 3 fours)

13. v Sri Lanka at Dambulla 4 October 2007 – England won by 65 runs
Toss: England
England 234–8 (50 overs) (O.A.Shah 82); Sri Lanka 169 (44.3 overs)

c D.P.M.D.Jayawardene b W.P.U.J.C.Vaas   1   (12 balls)

14. v Sri Lanka at Dambulla 7 October 2007 – England won by 2 wickets (D/L)
Toss: Sri Lanka
Sri Lanka 164 (41.1 overs) (T.M.Dilshan 70, G.P.Swann 4–34); England 164–8
(46.5 overs)

c K.C.Sangakkara b W.P.U.J.C.Vaas   0   (7 balls)

15. v Sri Lanka at Colombo (RPS) 10 October 2007 – England won by 5 wickets
Toss: Sri Lanka
Sri Lanka 211–9 (50 overs) (K.C.Sangakkara 69, L.P.C.Silva 67); England 212–5
(46.5 overs) (A.N.Cook 80, K.P.Pietersen 63*)

b C.R.D.Fernando   80   (123 balls; 6 fours)

16. v Sri Lanka at Colombo (RPS) 13 October 2007 – Sri Lanka won by 107 runs
Toss: Sri Lanka
Sri Lanka 211 (48.1 overs) (L.P.C.Silva 73); England 104 (29.1 overs)
(C.R.D.Fernando 6–27)

c K.C.Sangakkara b C.R.D.Fernando   28   (47 balls; 3 fours)

17. v New Zealand at Wellington 9 February 2008 – New Zealand won by 6 wickets
Toss: England
England 130 (49.4 overs); New Zealand 131–4 (30 overs)

b C.S.Martin   11   (26 balls)

**18. v New Zealand at Hamilton 12 February 2008 – New Zealand won by 10
wickets (D/L)**
Toss: New Zealand
England 158 (35.1 overs) (A.N.Cook 53); New Zealand 165–0 (18.1 overs)
(J.D.Ryder 79*, B.B.McCullum 80*)

run out (L.R.P.L.Taylor/B.B.McCullum)   53   (69 balls; 6 fours)

19. v New Zealand at Auckland 15 February 2008 – England won by 6 wickets (D/L)
Toss: England
New Zealand 234–9 (50 overs) (J.D.P.Oram 88); England 229–4 (44 overs)
(I.R.Bell 73, P.D.Collingwood 70*)

c C.S.Martin b J.D.P.Oram   9   (24 balls; 1 four)

20. v New Zealand at Napier 20 February 2008 – Match tied
Toss: New Zealand
England 340–6 (50 overs) (A.N.Cook 69, P.Mustard 83, K.P.Pietersen 50,
P.D.Collingwood 54*); New Zealand 340–7 (50 overs) (B.B.McCullum 58,
J.M.How 139)

b J.D.Ryder   69   (88 balls; 8 fours)

21. v New Zealand at Christchurch 23 February 2008 – New Zealand won by 34 runs (D/L)
Toss: New Zealand
England 242–7 (50 overs) (K.D.Mills 4–36); New Zealand 213–6 (37 overs) (B.B.McCullum 77)

lbw b D.L.Vettori   42   (70 balls; 4 fours)

22. v New Zealand at Lord's 28 June 2008 – New Zealand won by 51 runs
Toss: England
New Zealand 266–5 (50 overs) (S.B.Styris 87*, J.D.P.Oram 52); England 215 (47.5 overs) (O.A.Shah 69)

c B.B.McCullum b T.G.Southee   24   (38 balls; 3 fours)

23. v India at Cuttack 26 November 2008 – India won by 6 wickets
Toss: India
England 270–4 (50 overs) (K.P.Pietersen 111*, O.A.Shah 66*); India 273–4 (43.4 overs) (V.Sehwag 91, S.K.Raina 53*, S.R.Tendulkar 50, M.S.Dhoni 50)

c S.R.Tendulkar b Z.Khan   11   (15 balls; 1 four)

Alastair Cook in International Twenty20 Matches

International Twenty20 Career Record (2007)

M	I	NO	Runs	HS	Avge	S/R	100s	50s
2	2	0	24	15	12.00	96.00	–	–

1. v West Indies at The Oval 28 June 2007 – West Indies won by 15 runs
Toss: West Indies
West Indies 208–8 (20 overs) (D.S.Smith 61, M.N.Samuels 51); England 193–7 (20 overs) (P.D.Collingwood 79, D.R.Smith 3–24)

c D.J.Bravo b D.R.Smith   15   (16 balls; 2 fours)

2. v West Indies at The Oval 29 June 2007 – England won by 5 wickets
Toss: West Indies
West Indies 169–7 (20 overs) (C.H.Gayle 61); England 173–5 (19.3 overs) (O.A.Shah 55)

b D.B-L.Powell   9   (9 balls; 2 fours)

Full Career Record

First-class (2003–2009) – *up to and including England v Australia at The Oval 20–23 August 2009*

M	I	NO	Runs	HS	Avge	100s	50s
110	196	16	8104	195	45.02	21	45

List-A (Limited Overs matches) (2003–2009) – *up to and including Lancashire v Essex 23 May 2009*

M	I	NO	Runs	HS	Avge	100s	50s
58	57	4	1745	125	32.92	2	9

Test Centuries

160	v West Indies	Chester-le-Street	2009
139*	v West Indies	Bridgetown	2008/2009
127	v Pakistan	Manchester	2006
118	v Sri Lanka	Galle	2007/2008
116	v Australia	Perth	2006/2007
106	v West Indies	Manchester	2007
105	v West Indies	Lord's	2007
105	v Pakistan	Lord's	2006
104*	v India	Nagpur	2005/2006

One-day International Centuries

102	v India	Southampton	2007

INDEX